I0825089

FISHING WISDOM

FISHING WISDOM

A miscellany of angling anecdotes, facts & folklore

DOMINIC GARNETT

CONTENTS

INTRODUCTION

Fishing is a universally loved pastime. Anywhere humans find water they have the urge to fish. Everyone from our distant ancestors to today's children have gazed into the depths with fascination. Whether our aim is to catch a meal or just some peace and quiet, the pull is the same, and yet figuring out what makes fishing so precious to each of us can be as elusive as any fish.

Angling can be solitary or sociable, relaxing yet exciting. There is nothing in the world quite like that electric thrill of a fish on the line, and yet that tingle could be anything from a tiny minnow to a creature the size of a small car. Such is the endless challenge and diversity of angling.

Perhaps it is this variety that explains the sport's broad appeal. After all, fish do not care where you live, what language you speak, whether you are rich or poor, or anything else for that matter. Nor is age a barrier, and angling is one of those rare activities that both a small child and their 90-year-old great-grandparent can love equally. Wherever you are on your journey as an angler, I hope you find plenty to entertain and inspire you in these pages.

As an activity where sport, science and art overlap, it would be impossible to capture all of angling in just one volume, but you have a true miscellany (what a great word!) in your hands. We shall be wading into fishing's essentials alongside some of the wildest stories and catches ever. I make no apology for getting back to basics in some instances, however, because the very fundamentals of fishing are also its most important lessons.

We shall start with the roots of angling, which means not only how to choose tackle and catch fish but also how to gain maximum enjoyment. Even if you've fished for decades, I hope you'll be encouraged to find fresh questions and answers.

Section two then takes us into the process of understanding the places we fish. Anglers call this detective work watercraft, and with far more H_2O than land on planet Earth, it is a never-ending challenge. However, while mystery and sheer luck play a special part in angling, growing our knowledge can boost our enjoyment and success rate alike.

It's often said that fishing is about the chase as much as the catch, but the fish themselves are the stars of the show. Hence, in section three we'll take a look at wonderful, weird and iconic species, from wily trout to greedy bass. Who knows, some of the findings might change the whole way you look at fish!

In section four we look at angling crafts such as fly tying, as well as how to prepare and cook fish.

Last but not least, our final section delves into the wider world of angling culture. From wild legends to classic literature, our pastime represents an amazing mixed catch through the ages. Fishing is a timeless pleasure. On which note, I wish you happy reading and the very best of luck on your next fishing trip. Or 'Tight Lines' from one angler to another!

CHAPTER ONE

FISHING FUNDAMENTALS

'There are as many reasons why and ways to fish as there are people who do it.'
RUSSELL CHATHAM

'Fishing is a quest for knowledge and wonder as much as a pursuit of fish.'
PAUL SCHULLERY

'The charm of fishing is that it is the pursuit of what is elusive but attainable, a perpetual series of occasions for hope.'
JOHN BUCHAN

'The agony and the ecstasy is a six-year-old boy trying to go to sleep, knowing he's going fishing in the morning.'
FRANK P. BARON

Why do we go fishing? If the question seems simple, the possible answers are endless. For fun and excitement? To relax and connect with nature, far from our troubles? To enjoy time with family or friends? All of the above are valid answers, but it is always worth thinking about why we fish and what we're looking for, because the answer is likely to change throughout our life.

To take angling back to its very roots, the original reason to fish was simple: food! Our hunter-gatherer ancestors didn't get out there to admire a sunset or to prise young children away from video games. However, you can guarantee that the instinctive feeling of wonder and excitement was identical.

If we purely wanted a fish supper though, we would be better served by nets or other means. At some stage in human development, therefore, once we no longer needed to roam waterways with nets and spears, fishing became a sport rather than a simple means to an end. After all, even if you can get your fish from a supermarket, nothing can replace that magical tingle of a fish on a line. 'The tug is the drug!' as they say, even if many of us now carefully release our catch and have no grand designs beyond fun and fresh air. Recent studies also show that, far from being mere escapism, fishing is good for our mental and physical health. We'll explore this later. For now though, it's time to thread our line through the rod rings, head for the water and cast out into the fascinating world of angling.

HOOKS

WHY 'ANGLING'?

The term 'angling' derives from the old English word 'angle', meaning hook. Going back further, this can be traced to the Latin term 'angulus' (an angle or corner) and the Greek word 'ankos' (to bend). Use of the term 'angling' to describe fishing with rod and line, however, first crops up in the 1400s, notably when country sports writer Dame Juliana Berners wrote the *Treatyse of Fysshynge wyth an Angle*.

DEVELOPMENT OF HOOKS

Fishing hooks themselves go back a long way, although our ancestors first made them from bone or shell rather than metal. The earliest such purpose-made hook ever found came from Okinawa Island, Japan, and is over 22,000 years old. Jump to today, and tens of millions of dollars are spent on fish hooks every year worldwide. Compared to those of our ancestors, today's models look positively delicate, with barbless and circle hooks increasing in popularity as catch and release fishing grows.

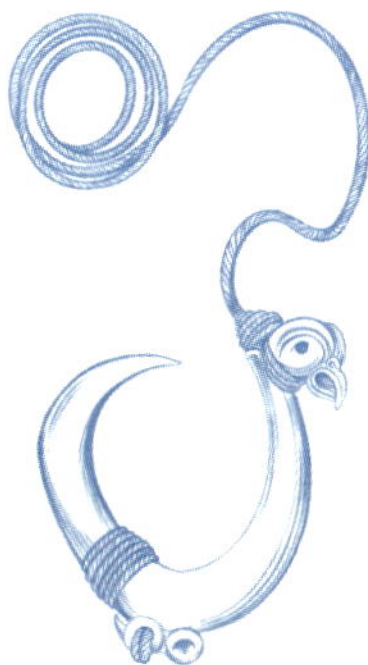
A Māori fish hook, made from bone

Today's mass-produced, ultra-sharp hooks are far more reliable than those of our forebears. The incredible range of types reflects the variety of fishing across the globe. To classify any hook, the lower the number on the packet, the larger it is, until we get to zero and the scale is reversed, hence a 4/0 is much larger than a 1/0. Fine-wire hooks for dry flies get as minuscule as a 32, which is smaller than an eyelash. At the other end of the spectrum, hand-sized hooks of size 10/0 and above are for sharks and big game. As for the most expensive hook ever, Mustad's 7761 'Super Marlin' pattern was nicknamed the 'Cadillac Hook'. This was not because it could tow an automobile (although it probably could) but because 1,000 of them cost the same as a brand-new Cadillac!

As with all tackle, the golden rule with hook choice is balancing with the task in hand, considering the size and type of fish, and the size of our bait, lure or fly. Barbless hooks are also growing in popularity as more of us release our catch, by choice or by law. Losing the barb is kinder to fish and to fingers and clothing. Where barbless hooks cannot be found, you can easily 'debarb' regular models with forceps or pliers.

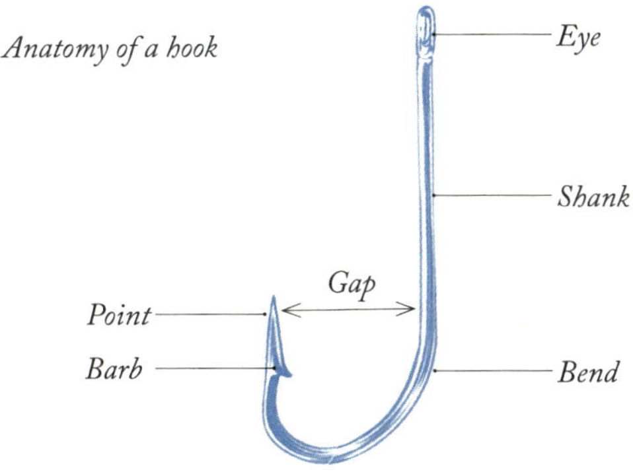

Anatomy of a hook

RODS

Humanity has made fishing rods or poles for thousands of years. Historically, people relied on wood, which is rarely preserved, and we don't know for certain when the first rods were made. Bamboo or 'split cane' was still the first choice for many anglers well into the 20th century. Around 1945, fibreglass rods started appearing, while enterprising anglers from the World War II generation also attached rings to military tank aerials to make rods.

Since the 1980s carbon rods have dominated, owing to the material's superior lightness and responsiveness. Unlike today's mass-produced blanks, the first carbon fishing rods could cost a month's wages. That's not to say the older materials don't retain their fans, who love the feel and smoother shock absorption of glass or cane for big fish.

However, some rules for selecting and caring for rods are near universal:

- What size and type of fish do I expect? The right rod will give us a healthy bend, but has the strength to land our intended catch efficiently.
- What will I cast and how far? Most rods have a weight rating that tells us what size lures, sinkers or lines it is designed for.
- How much space and reach do I need? A long rod of 10–12ft (about 3–4m) might be ideal for extra reach or casting heavy weights long distances, but on a small, bushy stream or crowded boat, a shorter model of 6–7ft (about 2m) would be a better fit.
- How many sections? The one- or two-part rod is the most universally useful because you can leave it rigged up and ready to fish (this gets messy with three parts!) Ultra-portable, multi-section rods are useful for the travelling angler.

- Use real-world retailers. In the Internet era, it's easy to buy the hype or order the wrong item. Support real-world tackle stores, where you can handle kit in person. Avoid cheap starter kits and telescopic rods.
- Clean and store with care – hard-wearing plastic tubes are the best way to keep rods safe in transit. Vehicle doors break as many rods as fish! Take a wet cloth and clean your rod rings, reel seat and other fittings regularly – and always rinse kit after using it in salt water.

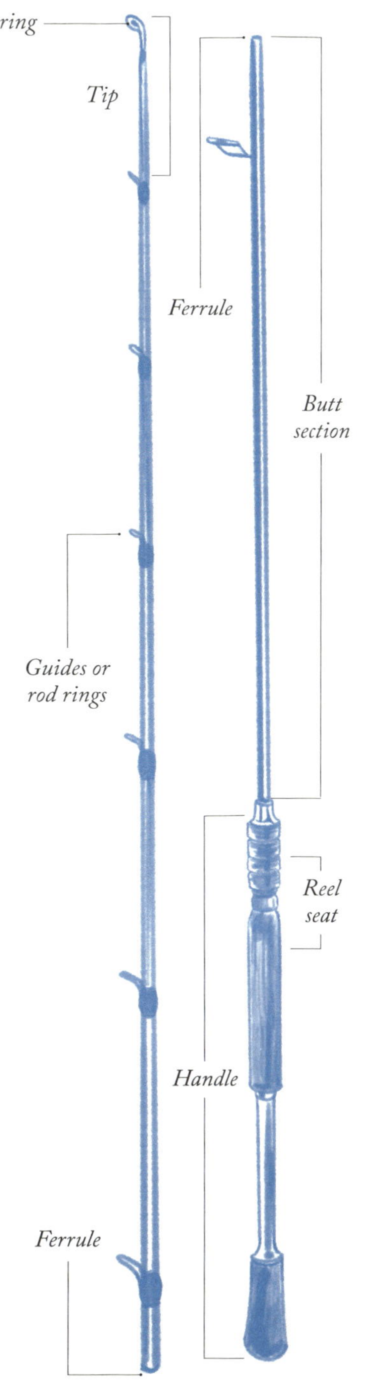

THE LONG AND SHORT OF IT: EXTREME RODS WORLDWIDE

There is no 'one size fits all' with fishing rods. The world's longest are the carbon poles used by European competition anglers, which can stretch to 59ft (18m)! As for the shortest, ice fishing rods can be under a foot – ideal if you're tackling a dinner-plate-sized hole on a frozen lake.

FISHING-ROD HACKS

REPLACING A TIP RING Nine times out of ten, when a rod breaks it is the tip that snaps. If the break is close to the very end of the rod, you can fix it. To get the tip ring off, heat carefully with a lighter and the resin will melt, allowing you to slide it free. Next, use sandpaper to file down the rod tip at the break and lose any splinters or cracks. Test for a snug fit before replacing the tip ring with a dab of superglue or epoxy.

STUCK OR LOOSE ROD JOINTS Rubbing candle wax to the 'male' join or ferrule is a quick way to restore a snug fit where parts have got loose. Stuck rod sections, though, are best tackled with a friend. Start by holding one half each, and pulling and twisting carefully in opposite directions. If this fails, get a third person to hold the rod at the join and wiggle in a circular motion as you pull. This should free any stubborn dirt or grit.

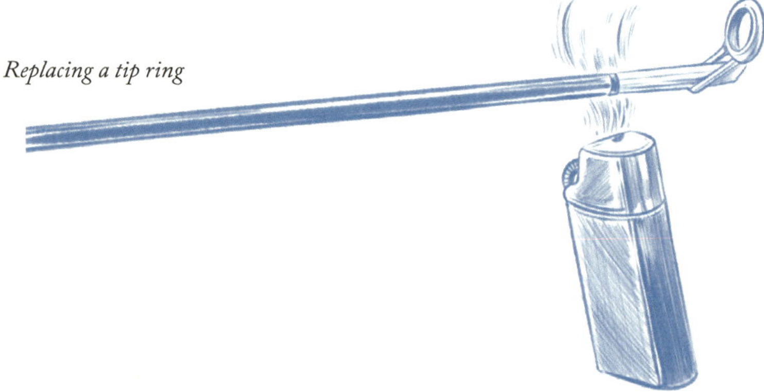

Replacing a tip ring

ROD CONTROL

There is far more to landing our catch than simply wrenching it in. When we hook a fish, the first task is to assess its size and power through the rod. Steady, unhurried pressure is best, and the aim is to avoid too much or too little force, while typically mirroring what the fish is doing (i.e. if it runs for a snag on your right, hold the rod firmly to the left).

The rod angle is critical, and while most anglers instinctively lift the rod high, this isn't very efficient except on smaller fish. In fact, pulling sharply upwards tends to make fish panic, presumably because the sky is not where they feel most at home.

With the rod held lower and to the side, the fight is far smoother and, as we bring the middle and lower rod into play, gives more power and control. In angling slang, this is sometimes called 'giving it the wood' – in other words, using the whole rod, not just the thin end.

REELS

We might take them for granted, but smooth, reliable modern fishing reels are a relatively recent invention. For most of history, humans used a simple pole and fixed line, until around 1200, when the Chinese crafted simple wooden spools with handles. Only centuries later did more advanced reels take shape, with the spinning or fixed spool style arriving in the early 1900s.

Images from the 13th century show Chinese fishermen using reels.

A French company called 'Mitchell' were the first to mass-produce these more advanced reels. At peak production, they made 25 tons (23 tonnes) of reels daily, turning out 33 million of the 'Mitchell 300' model alone.

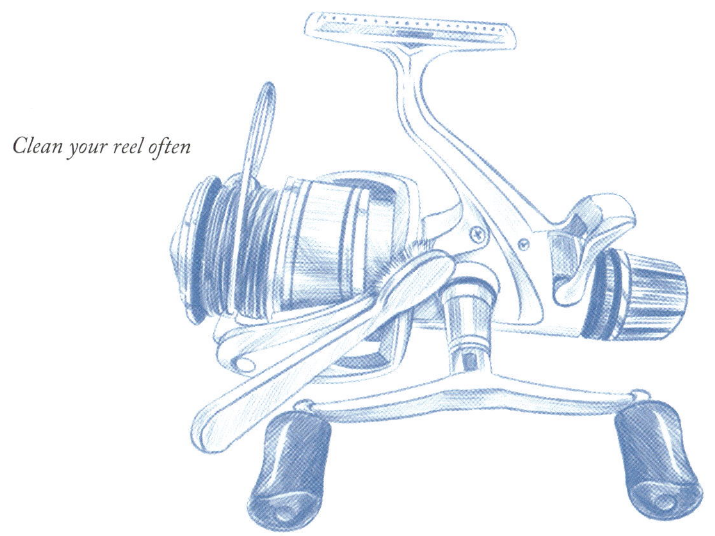

Clean your reel often

REEL CHOICE, CARE AND KEY FEATURES

Here are some key aspects:

- **Size and balance** are vital. A well-matched rod and reel should balance easily in the hand and not seesaw in one direction.
- **A reel's drag** controls how easily line is pulled off the reel, allowing a fish to run well before the line breaks. It's far better that you test this before fishing, rather than after hooking a monster fish that could snap you up!
- **Filling or spooling up** a reel without twisting your line is important. The easiest way, once you've tied the end to your reel, is to drop the spool of line in a bucket of water. Now reel under steady pressure, through a cloth, to keep things even.
- **Find the lip.** Your reel should always be filled just shy of the edge or 'lip' of the spool, so the line peels off easily when casting. Deep reels can be padded out with some tape or old line on first to avoid waste. One hundred yards (about 90m) or so is fine for most regular fishing.
- **Clean your reel** every so often with a wet cloth and use an old toothbrush for tricky nooks and stubborn dirt. Treating moving parts to purpose-made reel grease occasionally is also a good idea.

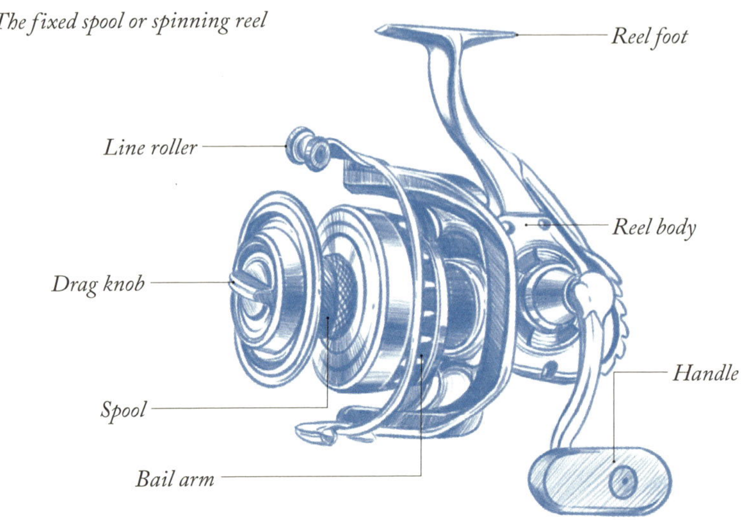

The fixed spool or spinning reel

THE FIXED SPOOL OR SPINNING REEL

The fixed spool or spinning reel is the easiest to use, and some anglers use little else. It has a bail arm that is flipped over to release line for casting, before being snapped back to 'engage' the line again. You'll also sometimes see 'closed face' versions with a cupped front and push-button line release, which are more limited but easy to use for novices.

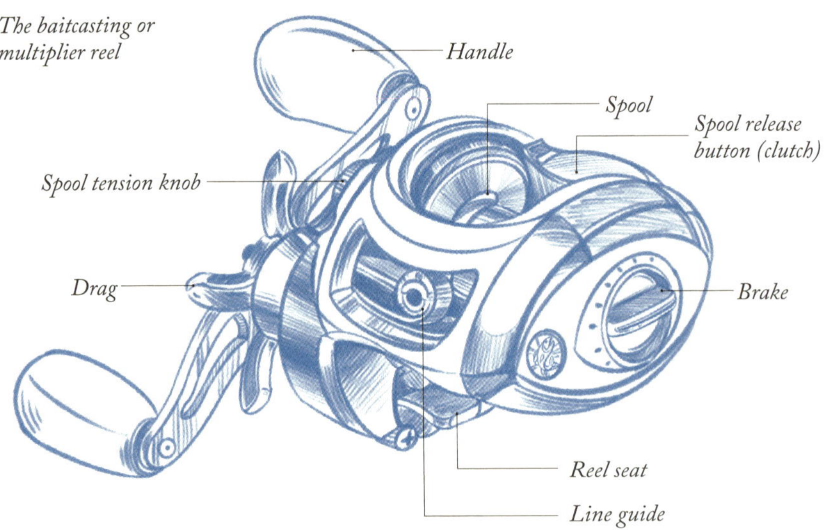

The baitcasting or multiplier reel

THE BAITCASTING OR MULTIPLIER REEL

This type of reel sits on top of the rod, rather than underneath, and is very popular with lure and specialist anglers. Although they take more getting used to, these reels offer increased casting distance and cranking power on large fish. Note the different position of the drag (often star shaped), and a line release switch instead of a bail arm.

The fly reel

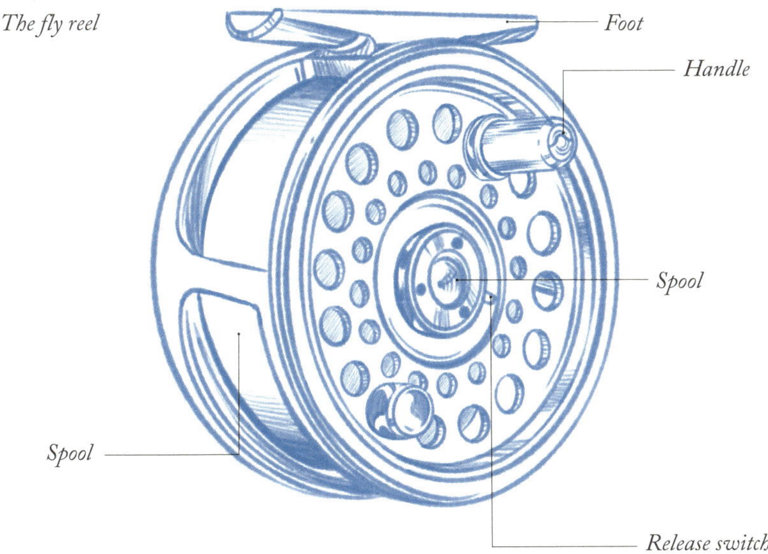

THE FLY REEL

A simple click knob controls the drag, while a switch releases the spool to change the line or deal with a tangle. For those too shy to ask, the stylish drilled holes make the reel lighter and help shed moisture.

LINES

Casting back in time, humanity has used everything from silk and horsehair to sheep intestines (aka catgut) as fishing line. Today's angler has line of a quality our ancestors couldn't dream of. There are four main kinds and, as with other tackle, the golden rule is to use balanced gear to meet our needs.

Monofilament, often simply called 'mono', is the most user-friendly all-round line. Made of nylon, its arrival in the 1930s changed fishing forever, making other materials obsolete. Strong, consistent and relatively cheap, it can be bought in a wide variety of strengths and colours.

Copolymer is a newer breed of mono made by fusing two or more materials. Thinner and more flexible than regular mono, it is ideal for things like end traces and fly tippets (the final section of line we knot onto our 'main line' to attach our fly, lure or baited hook).

Fluorocarbon is the new line on the block. Tougher than mono, it has better abrasion resistance, and with similar refractive properties to water it is less visible to fish. 'Fluoro' is also stiffer, less elastic and denser than regular line, meaning it is more inclined to sink.

Braided line or simply 'braid' is line made of woven synthetic materials. Offering great strength at a very thin diameter, it's perfect for long casts. With almost no stretch, it also has excellent 'feel' for detecting bites and imparting action into lures. It can, however, tangle easily in windy conditions.

HOW LONG DOES FISHING LINE LAST?

This varies depending on the type and how often you use it. It's always a good idea to check your line regularly for abrasion and kinking. Another good tip is to frequently remove the final two or three feet (about half a metre to a metre) on your reel lines, as this is where most wear and damage will occur.

TANGLES: A LESSON ON LIFE?

At times, fishing line seems to have a mind of its own, making knots that hardly seem possible. But while tangles cause frustration they can also be a blessing in disguise. After all, it rarely hurts to rest the water and let the fish settle.

TIP: BUY QUALITY AND STORE WITH CARE

As the vital connection between angler and fish, line is incredibly important and yet is often overlooked. First of all, always buy quality line and avoid bargains or items that might be old. Many lines deteriorate over time with exposure to UV light, so store in the dark where possible. A black football sock or stocking makes a good home for line spools.

And breathe.... Tangles happen to even the best anglers.

Tangles could even be said to be a metaphor for life's challenges. If we get angry and pull tight, situations invariably get worse. If we take a breath and carefully unpick things, however, most messes can be resolved – unless you have a true 'bird's nest', in which case you'll need scissors and a fresh start.

HOW SHOULD I DISPOSE OF LINE?

Discarded fishing line is no laughing matter. Modern materials do not biodegrade quickly and can harm wildlife. It's up to all anglers to minimise risk and dispose of line carefully. Line recycling programmes are increasing, while any line put in the rubbish can be cut into short sections that won't snare animals.

ALWAYS USE AN END TRACE

It's sensible to use an end trace (sometimes called a tippet or hook link) in almost all fishing. This means using a shorter length of line to attach your hook or lure that is weaker than the main line on the reel. Should this break off, this avoids leaving yards of discarded line.

BAIT FISHING

The art of using bait to catch fish might be as old as the hills, but the ways we can deliver food to fish are endless. We can anchor our offering to the bottom, present it in mid-water or even make it float, depending on where our quarry might expect a meal. We can detect bites with the tip of the rod, a floating indicator or simply via touch through our fingers.

KEY QUESTIONS FOR BAIT FISHING

- ***What* will the fish eat?** Our bait could be natural or artificial. Some fish are fussy or selective; others will accept almost anything edible. If we can find out what the fish naturally eat or what works for fellow anglers, so much the better.
- ***Where* are the fish feeding?** Are they on the bottom or up in the water? Close to the bank or further out? We can't always expect the fish to come to us.
- ***How* can we increase the odds of fish finding our bait?** There are many ways to boost our chances. In murky water, for instance, we might select something strong-smelling. In many cases 'loose feeding' or 'chumming' is key. This means introducing free bits of bait to draw fish in and get them confident. 'Little, often and accurate' is a good rule here – trickle in some free samples and fish are more likely to accept our hook bait.

BAIT-FISHING TECHNIQUES

FREE LINING This method is just a line and hook. It's best for close-range fishing, where you can spot your quarry – such as using floating bait for carp and other species.

FLOAT FISHING Using a floating bite indicator is a delightful way to fish. 'Pleasing in appearance, and even more pleasing in disappearance' is how angling scribe H. T. Sheringham described the appeal of the float (or 'bobber' to Stateside anglers). The right float is one that provides enough weight to reach the fish, but maintains sensitivity.

BOTTOM FISHING Also known as 'ledgering', a 'sinker' or weight is used to keep the bait on or near the bottom, which is often where big fish live. Bites are detected by watching the rod tip or using a bobbin, which rises or drops back when a fish takes the bait. If the bottom is silty or weedy, a good ruse is to anchor a buoyant or 'popped-up bait' so fish don't have to dig it out. Some rods have brightly coloured tips to aid bite detection when bottom fishing.

POLE FISHING A simple rod with a line fixed at the end remains a deadly way to fish. With no reel to tangle, it's also a superb method for beginners. Besides Huckleberry Finn types, it's also used by professional match anglers in Britain and Europe.

A bamboo pole and line is all Huckleberry Finn needed.

FISHING BAITS

The variety of food items that catch fish is endless. That said, fish vary hugely in their preferences. Just as a wild trout might only accept a mayfly during a thick hatch, a hungry shark will snaffle almost anything. One was found with an unopened tin of tuna fish in its stomach – presumably it couldn't find a can opener. Some offerings, however, are universal.

While some baits are well-known; others are quite surprising!

Worms are recognised as food by almost all fish. This is unsurprising because they get everywhere, from earthworms washed into rivers to the marine worms scoffed by bottom-dwelling sea fish. Start a home compost heap and you have free bait.

Maggots and grubs are equally deadly. Whether naturally occurring or purposely bred for fishing, most fish love them. Just watch where you store them – the family refrigerator is not recommended.

Bread is something fish accept almost anywhere they find humans. From small mullet to giant carp, they soon get a taste for it. One London angling club had to ban bread during post-World War II rationing when anglers' wives complained about too much disappearing as bait!

Fish often eat other fish, sometimes even their own kind. Whether it's a strip, chunk or whole small fish, predatory species will take it.

Prawns and shrimps are found in oceans and rivers all over the world. If you are on holiday and can't find bait, a few prawns are sure to tempt sea fish.

Pellets used in aquaculture are highly palatable to fish, whether they are fastened to the hook via a tiny bait band, or used ground up as an attractor.

Salted specials work as almost all animals love salt, which is a vital nutrient for all living things. Is this why bacon rind and tinned corn in brine are a hit with fish?

Groundbait, aka loose feed or chum, refers to anything edible we introduce to attract fish. It can be whole or chopped samples of our hook bait, or a specially made powder of ground seeds, grains, fishmeal and other ingredients, which is mixed with water, balled up and thrown in. You can make your own by grinding down bread or simply chopping up and throwing in a few worms. The effect on fish is akin to a fried food outlet on humans!

DEPOSITING FEED

Besides throwing by hand, anglers use various clever ways to get feed to fish. Sea anglers, for instance, sometimes lower a bag or cage of tasty scraps to draw fish such as sharks from all around. A catapult can project offerings well beyond throwing range. A swim feeder is a plastic or metal capsule used instead of a conventional weight or sinker, which deposits feed neatly, right next to our baited hook.

WORLD'S WEIRDEST BAITS

Sausages: You might get strange looks for using a chunk of hotdog, but various species like a meaty bait. It's tough skinned for the hook and fish love the salt and protein content.

Soap: The rich, fatty proteins of soap have made it a surprisingly good catfish bait in some locales.

Birds, frogs and mice: While most would balk at using bait of this sort, predatory fish such as pike and catfish eat a wide variety of small animals, live or dead. Even roadkill has been used.

Offal and body parts: The potent smell and high nutrition content of liver and other organs can be highly effective. Legend even has it that human body parts have occasionally found their way onto fishing hooks.

Bird droppings: Not a load of bull so much as a load of pigeon! Back in the 1980s Belgian anglers discovered the droppings of pedigree birds, fed on high quality seeds, produced a milky cloud highly attractive to fish.

FLY FISHING

Tricking fish into taking an artificial fly is arguably the most thrilling and elegant fishing style of all. Eschewing conventional means, fly fishers use special, weighted lines to cast an artificial fly to their quarry. Doing so accurately and in harmony with the elements is a true art form. It doesn't get more exciting than seeing a fish come up and steal a fly right in front of you! Nothing bends quite like a fly rod, either, so this way of fishing appeals to thrill seekers as much as purists.

Traditionally, fly fishing was all about sparkling waters and game fish such as trout and salmon. Today, however, it is a far broader church. Our artificial 'fly' needn't even be an insect. With a little imagination we can copy anything from a fleeing minnow to a crayfish to tempt anything from bass to tarpon. Studying and mimicking what fish eat adds a whole extra layer of creativity and understanding to angling.

Time flies: Humans have tricked fish using fur and feather since ancient times, but the first detailed account came from second-century Roman author Claudius Aelianus, who watched crafty Macedonians at work. 'They fasten red wool round a hook, and fit onto the wool two feathers which grow under a cock's wattles,' he wrote. 'They throw their snare, and the fish, attracted and maddened by the colour, comes straight at it.'

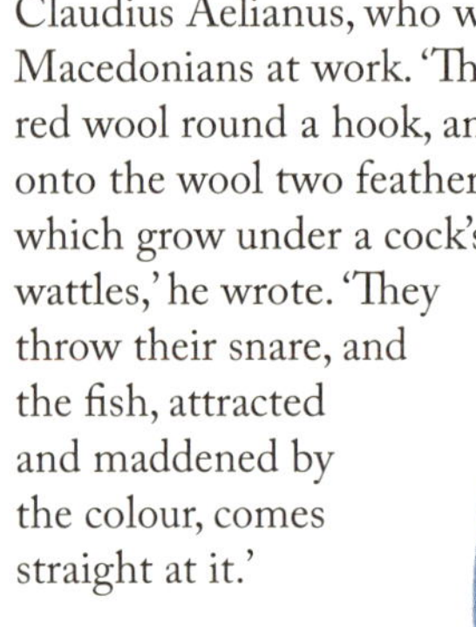

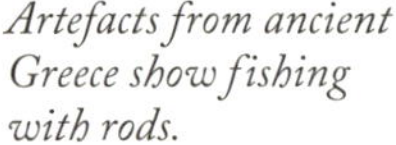

Artefacts from ancient Greece show fishing with rods.

Beaded Hare's Ear *Goddard Caddis* *Emerger Buzzer*

Many centuries later, countless fly designs (or patterns) and methods have evolved. From the chalk streams of England to the mountains of Japan, fly makers mimic an endless array of flies, bugs and prey items.

FAMOUS AND INFAMOUS FLIES

While a classic salmon fly can take hours to tie, many of the best flies are deceptively simple. Our ancestors used readily available materials to make wings, tails and other features – no prizes for guessing what a Hare's Ear or Pheasant Tail Nymph were made of. Particular materials are also used for practical effects. Hollow, naturally buoyant deer hair, for example, lends itself perfectly to floating and surface waking flies such as the Goddard Caddis and Muddler Minnow. To create the opposite effect and add 'bling', others used tiny metallic beads to create deadly, sinking flies, as the Japanese first did over 300 years ago.

Other special effects include the modern 'emerger' style fly, perhaps the most famous being the Klinkhamer. Mimicking a fly in the precarious stage of sitting half in, half out of the water during hatching, this represents the perfect easy meal for a fish.

As for the oddest fly ingredients, some are stranger than fiction. The Tupps Indispensible was made by an English butcher using the pinkish, waxy hairs from ram's testicles. The Collie Dog is self-explanatory, while some salmon anglers went even further by using intimate hair from their wives, convinced that female pheromones were irresistible to fish.

FLY-FISHING STYLES AND CONCEPTS

From the simple concept of fooling fish with an artificial insect, fly fishing has evolved a wide variety of styles and methods. We will deal with actual fly life in our watercraft chapter, but here are some common terms and techniques.

The moment of truth: will the fish accept or refuse our fly?

DRY FLY FISHING Traditional, elegant and visually exciting, it was heavily refined on England's River Test, where it gained cult status, with some clubs even banning sunk flies. The aim is simple enough: the angler tries to tempt fish by 'matching the hatch' with realistic floating imitations of insects the fish expect to find.

NYMPHING OR WET FLY FISHING When fishing with wet flies, anglers attach a weighted fly to their line, which sinks into the feeding zone of fish on a river or stream. There are various ways to present a sinking fly: most often either on its own or beneath a dry fly or indicator of some kind. Various styles of wet fly fishing exist. Loch style originates on the breezy lakes of Ireland and Scotland and uses a 'team' of three or four bushy, traditional flies. Euro nymphing involves an extra long rod and leader to provide close control of heavy nymphs on rivers.

STREAMER OR LURE-STYLE FLIES Fish rarely get big by only eating delicate little flies. A streamer (sometimes confusingly called a 'lure') doesn't imitate an insect, but bigger, juicier prey such as a minnow or leech. These flies tend to be fished in a vigorous, provocative style, which can make for viscerally thrilling sport for bass, pike and other species besides trout.

DEAD DRIFT OR INDUCED TAKE? Anglers on running water tend to try to let their fly travel perfectly naturally at 'dead drift' – which is a term meaning the same speed as the current. This is sensible, because a fly that behaves unnaturally or against the current tends to be refused. However, there are notable exceptions. Prey items such as caddis, grasshoppers and shrimps will often kick or make some commotion. Tweaking our fly to trigger the fish is known as the 'induced take'.

CARBON COPY OR GENERAL FIT? It's easy to get hung up on specific flies and prey items, but we don't always need to be ultra fussy. Fish don't count legs or look up the Latin names of mayflies! If it looks edible and natural, the chances are they will have it. Creating perfect copies of flies is fun and rewarding, therefore, but many of our most successful patterns are general fit. A scruffy-looking Hare's Ear, for instance, might vaguely resemble a freshwater shrimp, a caddis larva or nothing in particular. Rather than saying 'perfect copy of X' the message is 'eat me!'

MIMIC OR PROVOKE? Fish do not always take flies out of hunger. Sometimes they bite from natural curiosity, aggression or sheer instinct, in the same way even a well-fed house cat will attack a toy. Certain flies are out and out stimulators, designed to trigger aggression. After all, fish aren't always feeding. Atlantic Salmon, for instance, don't eat at all in freshwater and must be provoked.

A classic salmon fly is designed to provoke a response rather than copying a natural insect.

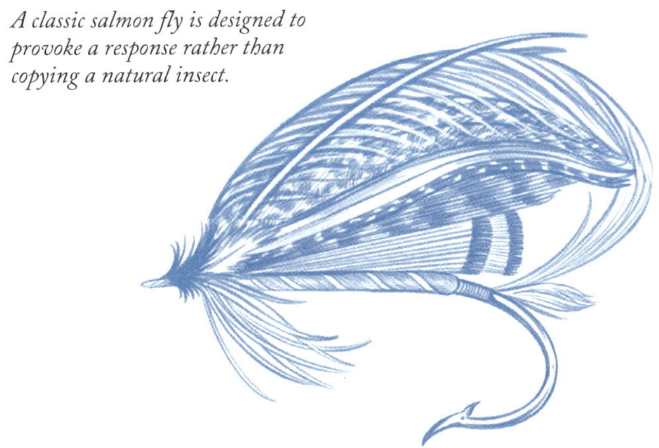

SINGLE FLY OR DUO? While fishing just one fly is beautifully simple, two can be better still. We can pair up two wet flies together or even two dries, while an even more useful setup is a buoyant dry fly with a sinking fly underneath, secured by a foot or two of line straight to the bend of the dry fly hook. Doubling up allows us to try flies of different sizes and colours – just be sure to put the heavier fly last to avoid tangles.

LURE FISHING

As lures represent 'baitfish' and other prey items, this branch of angling is all about predatory species, which tend to be the fastest, most aggressive and exciting fish. Lures can be made from wood, metal or plastic. They can be large or small and can imitate anything from tiny fry to a foot-long (30cm) mullet.

LURE TYPES AND THEIR ORIGINS

Lure fishing is anything but new. Metal lures are among the earliest, and well over a thousand years ago Nordic people created what we'd now call spoons. In Finland, these were cut from the sides of copper cooking pots, the curved shape providing a seductive wobble. Spinners would eventually evolve from these, featuring a metal blade that spins around a solid body. Wooden lures, broadly classed as plugs, came next. There is evidence that early versions were produced in China as early as the 10th century.

Metal minnows and creature-style lures hit English tackle shops in the late 18th century. Lure fever hit the USA next, where 19th-century hard-bodied lures achieved different effects, from diving, wiggling crankbaits to surface waking topwaters or poppers. All these innovations began as handmade versions from enterprising locals. James Heddon, for instance, carved his first surface poppers from bits of broomstick after watching a bass hit a piece of

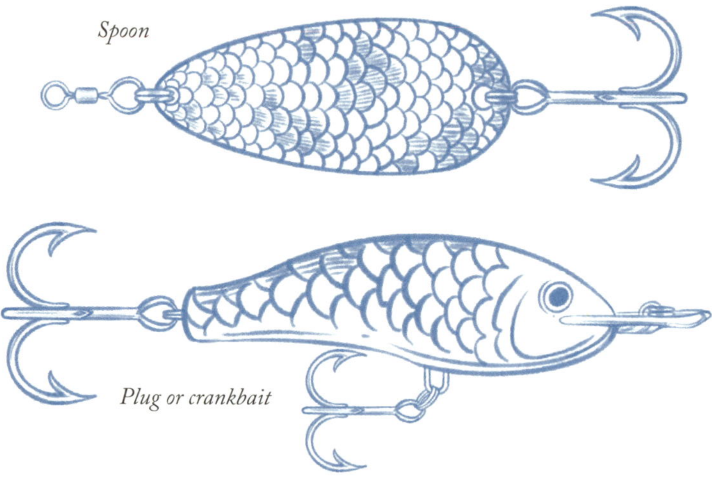

wood he'd thrown into a pond. Back in Europe, Lauri Rapala hand-produced lifelike minnows with balsa wood and a knife, using the foil from chocolate wrappers to add flash. Last but not least, we have soft plastic lures and jigs. Produced in endless colours and sizes, from lifelike shads to worms and crawdads, these continue to evolve, fooling fish and anglers alike.

THE WORLD'S MOST EXPENSIVE LURE

Vintage fish catchers fetch big bucks at auction, but none come close to the Million Dollar Lure, created by MacDaddy from platinum, gold and diamonds. Amazingly, it was even used for a brief trial, albeit with a 500lb (about 225kg) steel leader and a hefty insurance policy.

LURE FISHING STYLES

Casting lures from shore or boat is a fun, active way of fishing for novices and experts alike. The way we bring our lure in (called the retrieve) can vary greatly, however. Here are some common terms and ideas to bring lures to life.

STRAIGHT RETRIEVE – Keep reeling straight and steady!

WALK THE DOG – A popular style with topwaters and gliding lures such as jerkbaits, the angler uses a series of sharp flicks of the rod tip, making the lure dart attractively from side to side.

SINK AND DRAW – An erratic style of pulling the lure a yard or two (1–2m) at a time before pausing. It is deadly, with soft plastics, jigs or spoons that wiggle or flutter as they fall. Predators will often hit on the pause.

TROLLING – Trailing a lure behind a boat.

JIGGING – An up and down motion. This can also be done directly underneath a boat or structure such as a wall or jetty (vertical jigging).

DROP SHOTTING – Rigging a lure just off the bottom, coming off the line at a right angle just above a sinker. Originally invented by US anglers for small lures in deep water, it's also loved by European perch and zander catchers.

LRF/ULTRALIGHT LURE FISHING – Slender modern rods can cast lures as tiny as 0.01oz (0.5g) in weight. Scaling down can lead to thrilling sport with miniature predators in salt and freshwater alike.

TACKLING UP

With the bewildering array of rods, reels and tackle on show these days, it's easy to feel bamboozled by fishing kit. But what are the basic requirements of any fishing trip? Here's a checklist of things we wouldn't want to be without.

- A rod, reel and line suitable for your chosen method and species
- Flies, lures, hook, sinkers and other terminal tackle (plus spares)
- Fishing permits/licences – always check what you need
- A waterproof pouch for your wallet, keys and phone
- Weatherproof boots or waders
- Polarising sunglasses, for eye protection and fish spotting
- Suitable outdoor clothing to reflect the season and weather
- Water, food, sunblock (a pack of spares can 'live' in your vehicle)
- A landing net is a must to land larger fish – be optimistic!
- Forceps or another hook removal device
- Scissors, hook sharpener
- A tool to dispatch fish, plus a cool bag or container, should you intend to take any of your catch home.

GOLDEN RULES FOR FISHING TACKLE

- Balanced tackle is a must. Your rod and line should be strong enough to handle the conditions and fish you encounter, while retaining sensitivity.
- Keep it tidy! Rod straps, cases and boxes keep your kit safe and organised. Give items like unhooking gear and scissors a safe, permanent home so you always know where to find them.
- Stay light and mobile – too much gear can cramp your mobility. The angler who carries less can move spots faster and concentrate with fewer distractions.
- Always carry spares of your favourite lures, flies and bait. Wise fly fishers, for instance, swear by taking three of a favourite pattern: one to use, one to lose and one to give to a friend.
- Check, clean and dry your kit between trips to prevent the spread of unwanted parasites and invasive species. Drying out nets and waders in the sun will kill most of them.

WHAT KIND OF ANGLER AM I?

Everywhere you go in the world, angling has both similarities and unique local variations. Today's methods have evolved over many centuries across myriad cultures, and today's connected world is blurring boundaries and ideas more than ever. It's also worth saying that no approach is inherently superior to any other. All are valid and the way we fish should be a personal decision, free of snobbery or needless comparison. Which ethos describes you best?

- The **pleasure angler** fishes just for the heck of it. The best reason of all?
- The **purist** or **traditionalist** loves the craft, culture and history of angling. He or she wants to catch fish in the most enjoyable or artful way possible. They often love making their own tackle.
- The **species hunter** prizes the variety of fish both great and small, and is rather like a collector. How many species is it possible to catch?
- The **trophy hunter** or **specimen angler** is one who becomes dedicated to seeking large or special fish, often of a particular species.
- The **competition angler** loves the thrill of contest and wants to test their skills against fellow anglers as well as fish.

CHAPTER TWO

WATERCRAFT

'Most of the world is covered by water. An angler's job is simple: Pick out the best parts.'
CHARLES WATERMAN

'There is nothing like the thrill of expectation over the first cast in unfamiliar waters.'
CHARLES DUDLEY WARNER

'Beginners often believe the myth of patience. The best anglers I know are somewhat impatient. If they aren't catching fish they try something different.'
JOHN BARSNESS

'The two best times to fish is when it's raining and when it ain't'.
PATRICK F. MCMANUS

Almost anywhere in the world you find water, you will find fish. But while most humans just admire the surface of a pretty lake or meandering river, anglers get an invitation to explore another world. For anyone with fishing in their blood, understanding this realm of tides and currents, shallows and deeps, is an endless fascination. We call this process watercraft.

Figuring out different fishing locations is a pursuit that can last a lifetime. Besides observation and logic, it requires instinct and imagination. Curiosity is more of a virtue than patience in this regard, and the angler's mind is brimming with questions. Where are the fish hiding? What does the bottom look like? What just made that splash?

This chapter not only answers some of these questions, but also invites you to ask your own. After all, rivers, lakes and seas are dynamic, living environments and every day is different. On that basis, we should always be wary of taking the latest trend or article we've read as gospel. Successful fishing is not like following a set recipe, but more a case of thinking on your feet and developing your own ideas and observations. Hence, while it's always useful to listen to successful anglers, finding your own answers is the greatest satisfaction of all. So, whether you want to track down the fish of a lifetime or just suss out your local stream, it's time to look beneath the surface.

UNDERSTANDING WATER

Beyond maps and guides, getting access and permission to fish is vital for any angling trip. Always find out any rules, and never just assume it's fine to fish. The very process of finding out who runs the fishing is almost always helpful in itself, especially if you ask the right questions. In fact, being bold and talking to fellow anglers will set you in good stead anywhere in the world.

Websites and forums can be useful in this regard, but real-world fishing clubs and tackle shops are an even better source of information for initial 'digging'. After all, unlike social media users who may have no intention of sharing favoured spots or methods, these businesses want you to catch fish. If you succeed, you'll soon be back for another permit, some fresh bait or a new rod.

Even experienced anglers cut corners or forget to ask for help. Fishing is a lifelong process, however, and every new spot is a fresh mystery. Hence, if we just guess or assume we know it already, a lot can be missed. We'll deal with some 21st-century tools next, but old-fashioned sources of knowledge are still invaluable, including coaches and guides. These experts have priceless experience and local tips that might take years to discover on your own.

From babbling brooks, village ponds to tidal rivers and vast reservoirs, how can we understand the water we fish in better?

SOME USEFUL TOOLS

POLARISING GLASSES Even in the 21st century, our eyes and feet are still our best assets for finding the best fishing. Polarising sunglasses cut through glare, helping us spot underwater features as well as fish far more easily.

WADERS AND IMMERSIVE GEAR Where safe to do so, getting 'into the drink' is always revealing. Water is deceptive to the eye, after all, but less so to the touch. Waders help us access places we cannot reach from the bank, or you could even don a mask and snorkel where appropriate.

DEPTH PLUMBS OR PLUMMETS Use a float and a special weight called a depth plumb or plummet to check the water's depth. This is a heavy weight with a cork base for the hook. Drop it down and see what you can find.

MAPS AND APPS Digital tools are another handy way to get to know fishing spots. Phone apps provide up-to-date river levels, weather and even catch reports, while Google Earth is an amazing way to scan large areas of water in seconds. Real-world maps can be just as good, especially those showing depths and features.

FISHFINDERS AND CAMERAS Modern fishfinders can provide amazing detail of what lies beneath, while some anglers even use underwater cameras. However, tech is not essential – and as well as adding knowledge it can also take away from our experience. An electronic finder could be a godsend on a vast lake or at sea, for example, but how much mystery do we want to remove? Do we want our time spent looking at nature or a screen? It's your call.

LOGS AND DIARIES Whether you use your phone or a notebook, keeping a fishing diary is always worthwhile. Noting down things like weather, methods tried and bite times is incredibly helpful for future reference. Whether you are successful or not, patterns and lessons are sure to emerge.

HOW TO READ A RIVER

With constant motion and mystery, rivers are the spiritual home of many anglers. From tiny streams to giant tidal waterways, they hold endless life from tiny mayflies to mighty salmon. While every river is unique, all share typical characteristics, and the angler's understanding grows the more time they spend walking, looking and fishing. So what are some typical features?

RIFFLES are shallow, fast-flowing areas, where water rushes over stones. Although lacking depth for larger fish, these well-oxygenated places are rich in the insect life fish and other creatures depend on. Besides good places to see what's on the menu, they're also often safe places to cross a river.

RUNS or **GLIDES** are smooth sections of water with steady current and depth. Various residents thrive here, especially oxygen-loving species. Fish will tend to sit facing upstream, or into the current, alert for food pushed towards them in the flow. Watch for them rising to take flies.

POOLS are wider, deeper spots where fish find extra food and shelter. They can be ideal for larger creatures that need more space or migratory species seeking sanctuary on their journey.

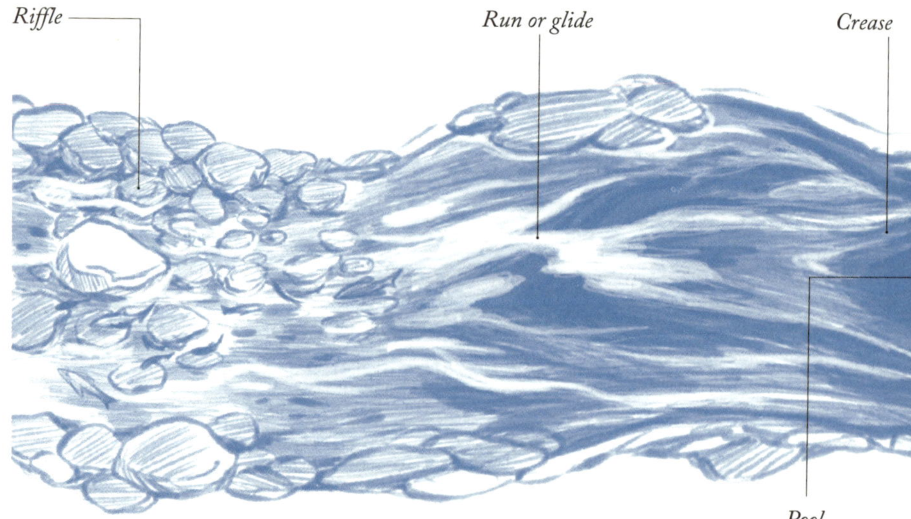

CORNERS or **BENDS** on any river produce interesting effects. These areas often provide fish with resting places out of the flow, while currents can also scour out deeper hidey-holes and undercuts.

EDDIES are spots where whirlpools form or the flow turns back on itself. Food often gets trapped here, so these are prime feeding grounds.

CREASES are zones where fast and slower water meet, literally giving the surface a 'creased' look. Fish love places where they can save energy by sitting just out of the main flow, yet close enough to dart out and grab passing prey.

SNAGS and **COVER** are terms anglers use to describe natural or artificial features fish like. This could mean a weed bed, an overhanging tree, or even a piece of scrap metal. Anything that provides cover, food or a vantage point could be a hotspot.

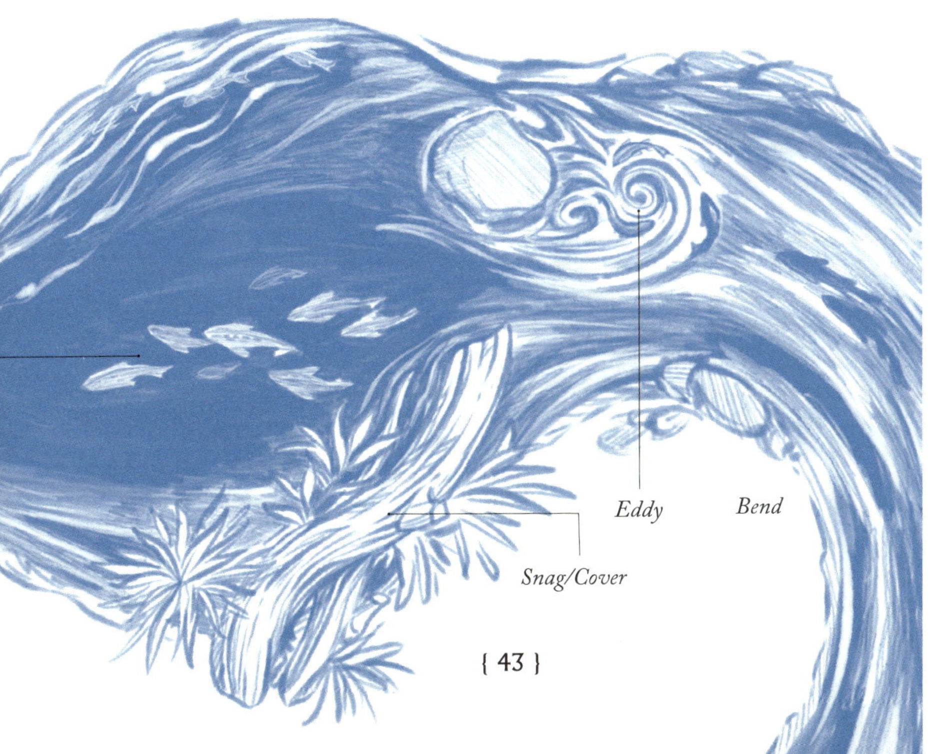

HOW TO READ A LAKE

Unlike a river, with its rolling currents, bends and pools, lakes can be a harder mystery to unravel. Many of the most interesting features, such as depth changes, sunken plateaus and gravel bars, are invisible from the surface. Nevertheless, there are lots of useful common features we can identify. Don't take the term 'stillwaters' too literally, however, because lakes are also dynamic, changing environments.

BAYS are shallower or more secluded areas of lakes, often in the corners. Weedy and more sheltered than the deeps, they provide fish with places to feed, hide and spawn.

ISLANDS are often fish magnets for the sanctuary they provide – especially if there is cover or deep water nearby.

STRUCTURE and **COVER** are words to describe all manner of physical features, from sunken logs to lily beds and even wrecked boats. Anglers love them as much as the fish.

INLETS are spots where another water source enters a lake, often bringing in food and oxygen. They can be hotspots for feeding fish, not to mention migration lanes for those on the move.

POINTS are spots where the bank juts out prominently. Fish often follow such contour lines or are funnelled by them, making them good spots for the angler to intercept their quarry.

DEEPS AND DROP-OFFS are areas where the bottom plunges away. Some fish species prefer deeper water, or gravitate here at certain times to find stable temperatures. Depth changes in general tend to attract fish, whether it's contour lines they patrol for food, or sudden 'drop-offs' that provide ambush points.

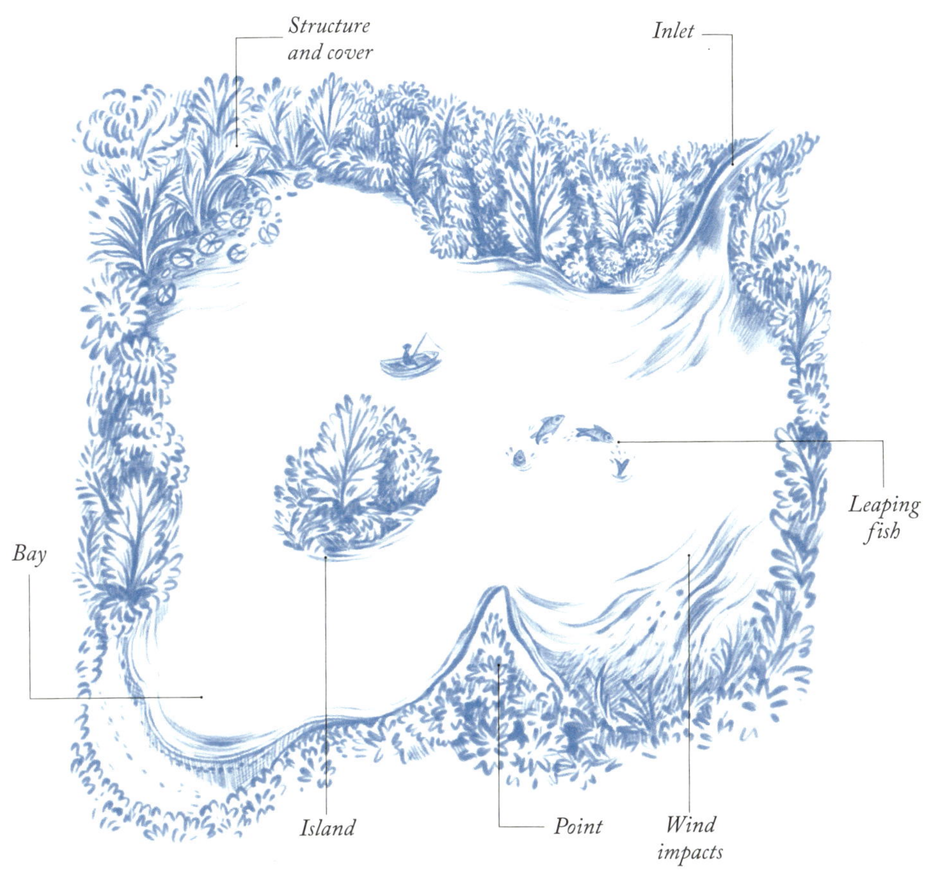

WIND IMPACTS So-called wind lanes are flat spots in among ruffled water, where creatures such as insects get trapped. Other wind impacts include 'colour change' zones where the water has been stirred up or food is concentrated by a prevailing breeze. Fish are sure to capitalise.

LEAPING, CRUISING OR RISING FISH are all encouraging signs. We'll deal with specific clues shortly, but on most lakes dawn and dusk are peak times to witness activity. Binoculars are worth taking on large waters.

UNDERSTANDING THE SEASHORE

Vast in size compared to most freshwater settings, the ocean can be a daunting prospect. However, it's also this very scale and dynamism that make saltwater thrilling and mysterious. Even faced with the biggest stretch of coast, however, we can break things down into smaller, identifiable features.

ROCKS AND ROCKPOOLS contain myriad food items for fish, from crabs and prawns to shellfish. Visit at low tide to find likely hotspots and see what's lurking in rockpools and gulleys.

OPEN BEACH areas are often the hardest to assess for fishing potential. Even seemingly featureless sand and grit conceal life, however, such as worms, shrimps and sand eels. Some species, especially flatfish, prefer open ground. In spots popular with swimmers, try night fishing.

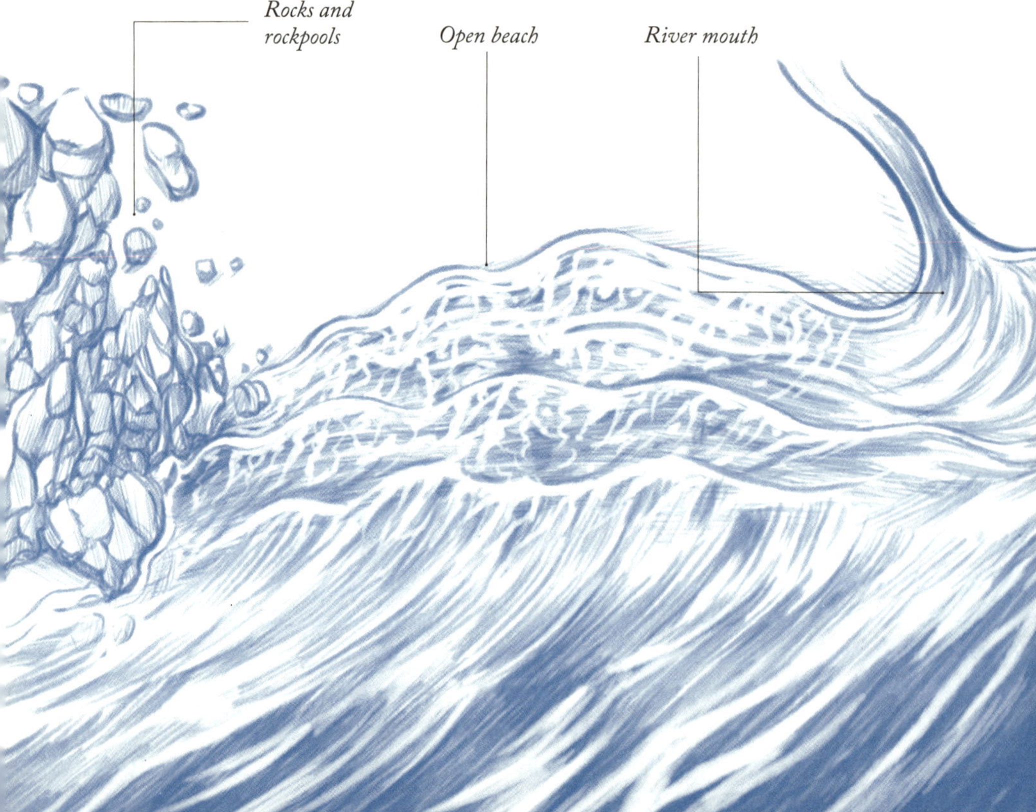

INTERTIDAL ZONES are always worth exploring, with various fish preferring different states of tide and seasons. Don't always assume they are far out! At the biggest spring tides or following a storm, for instance, even big fish will come in to devour dislodged prey and access new feeding grounds.

RIVER MOUTHS are prime areas for resident fish and migratory species alike, including those capable of living where fresh and salt water meet, such as bass, mullet and flounder. Look out for tide-rips and natural larders like worm and shellfish beds.

HARBOURS offer shelter to humans and fish alike, and are great places to try lighter tackle or to escape rough weather. Long casts are often unnecessary, with rock-loving species living right under sea walls. Do check any rules and don't get in the way of working boats.

PIERS AND SEA DEFENCES offer the angler a shot at deeper water and structure without having to cast to the horizon. Fish are often attracted to features such as pier legs, breakwaters and harbour lights.

SIGNS OF FISH

One of the wonders of lakes, rivers and seas is that we never quite know what we'll see next. Nature presents us infinite visual clues, if we are only attentive enough to look. One way to think of it is a kind of sign language we can learn.

BUBBLES are one way bottom-feeding fish betray their presence. Trails of smaller, fizzing bubbles tend to mean active fish are stirring up the bottom, whereas occasional, larger bubbles may be a false alarm, caused by gas escaping from the river or lake-bed.

CLOUDING OR DISCOLORATION can be another sign of bottom feeders at work. Look out for what look like slow-motion explosions of silt or sand as fish snuffle about. In the case of a large shoal, you might find a discoloured patch of many square yards.

SWIRLS, BOILS OR MOVING PLANTS are other ways fish give themselves away. Large customers can be quite clumsy when passing through shallow water or cover. On occasion, fish will even bash into foliage to dislodge food items like snails and fly larvae.

ROLLING AND TURNING Fish are active for various reasons. On a stony river, for instance, you might see fish flash and turn as they intercept invertebrates. Fish that filter feed on the bottom will also sometimes roll on the surface to clear dirt out of their gills.

LEAPING can be for several reasons. Salmon, trout and other migratory species will jump to ascend obstacles on their journey. At other times, large fish will jump and slap down on the water to rid themselves of parasites. Smaller fish will leap vigorously to escape predators or express danger to shoalmates.

FEEDING CLUES

Another way fish often betray their presence is in the rise forms they make when taking insects. This is especially true of trout, but not confined to game fish. These indications range from very subtle to violently obvious. Identifying what's going on can take a little practice but is both exciting and helpful to the angler.

THE BULGE Fish don't always shatter the surface as they feed. Should they be taking insect larvae or hunting fry just below the top, the watchful angler may see just slight bulge or a small, flat spot form among the ripples.

GENTLE RISES occur when fish are picking carefully at tiny morsels, such as midges or small mayflies. Don't always assume a small rise form is a small fish, however!

HEAD AND SHOULDER RISE FORMS signal fish feeding confidently. You may well spot this happening during a good hatch of insects. In this mood, the whole head and shoulder of the fish may appear, or fins bristle at the surface.

SPLASHES OR SLASH TAKES mean fish feeding on larger or clumsier prey. Morsels like crane flies, grasshoppers or caddis are not delicate meals; they often wake or splutter and a fish will grab them aggressively. You might also see small prey fish flipping clear as predators attack, one of the most thrilling sights in angling!

WHERE DID YOU GO? As a general rule, when we see rise marks on the water, the fish is often slightly further away than we think, especially on a river. This is because the rings formed travel with the current- and this imprint may travel a few feet. In most cases, it's not advisable to drop a fly or bait right on a fish's head and risk alarming it. It is far more natural to let it drift gently into striking range.

FISH PREY

Looking at the endless flies and prey items in and around water, it's easy to get confused, but we needn't be bug experts to cash in. A little observation goes a long way – and if we can make a rough match in size or colour, or perhaps even fill a bait tub, we're already winning. Starting with insects, we can classify most into just four main categories:

MAYFLIES are found worldwide in various guises, and often indicate river health. While the larva tend to live a year in stones and grit, adults last just a single day, to mate and die. The largest and most iconic, *Ephemera danica*, is large, cream or greenish coloured and unmistakable. Dozens of smaller mayfly types are confusingly called 'olives', including the March brown, pale watery and blue winged olive (BWO). Mayflies have a dainty look, with long trailing tails and wings held up and back, which explains why some call them upwings.

Mayfly

Caddis fly

CADDIS FLIES, aka **SEDGE FLIES**, are another common insect in freshwater habitats worldwide. Watch any lake or stream on a summer evening and you'll probably see fluttery, moth-like creatures. These are adult caddis flies, which have emerged after many months on the bottom, where most build tiny 'cases' out of grit and sand. Adults have a messy, busy appearance and often provoke splashy rises.

A fly made to mimic the larva of 'buzzers'.

BUZZERS, aka **CHIRONOMIDS**, are a huge family of midges and similar insects that tend to be small and drab or dark. The name 'buzzer' comes from the high-pitched buzzing sound they make in flight. Thriving even in poor habitats and hatching all year, they are a key food source for countless freshwater fish and animals. Surface and midwater cruisers love to take them as they ascend and hatch, but bottom feeders also take the larva, sometimes called bloodworms.

TERRESTRIALS is a blanket term for insects and critters that are not born in water, but get there by accident. This includes beetles, ants, caterpillars and even grasshoppers. Fish like bass and chub love to snaffle these as much as trout and it's awesome fun to use a lifelike copy.

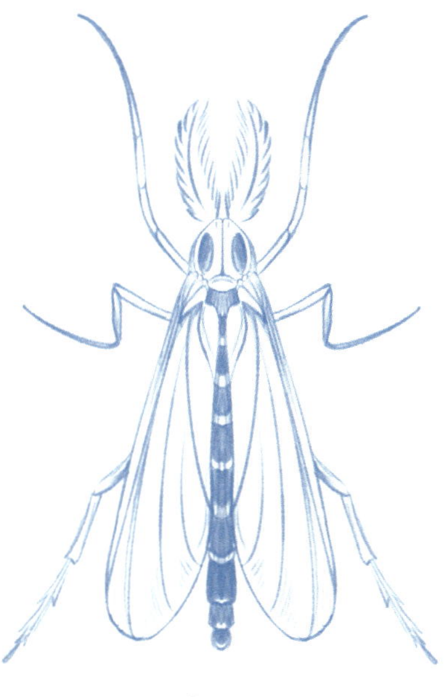

Buzzer

Grasshopper

FRY and **JUVENILE FISH** are staple foods for predators. It's a fish-eat-fish world out there, and many species will switch to flesh at certain times of year, such as when fry are abundant. If you can identify the going fodder fish, this can help inform lure and fly choices.

SNAILS, SHRIMPS, LEECHES AND OTHER MINI BEASTS form an endless variety of prey, wherever you fish, which can be imitated with the right lure or fly, or even harvested as bait.

HOW DO WE FIND OUT WHAT FISH ARE EATING?

It's all well and good talking about 'matching the hatch' but it can take a little detective work to identify what is on the menu. The best way of all is to dip in directly, and that can mean using some basic tools, besides just our hands and eyes. A fine-meshed net is ideal for running through rock pools, or the shallows of a river or lake. Turning over stones is another good way to find fish prey; don't forget a bait bucket for any useful goodies! Other likely places to find evidence are the windswept corners of a lake, where insects are blown, or even spiders' webs close to the bank. Fly anglers can benefit by taking hi-res photos to inform their creative copies at the vice. Last but not least, if you take a fish for the table, it could be worth doing a brief 'autopsy'.

An artificial mouse, fashioned from deer hair and leather.

THE WILDER ITEMS THAT FISH EAT

A list of the prey items ingested by fish would make a jaw-dropping book in its own right! For larger and more aggressive fish, very little is off limits. If it's edible and fits inside those jaws, down it goes. Sharks and catfish have produced the craziest finds of all, but even less formidable fish often surprise us. Fish are naturally curious, after all, and with no hands to pick up and inspect the things they find, their main means to 'test' dinner is to open wide.

RODENTS quite often find their way into rivers and lakes. Predatory fish like trout and bass will happily take a mouse, and some intrepid anglers even create lifelike copies.

BIRDS are also on the menu, and not just chicks. Pike and catfish have been found with moorhens, ducks and pigeons down their throats, while the giant trevally will catch seabirds in mid air (see 'Fish vs Birds' on YouTube).

REPTILES AND AMPHIBIANS Frogs, newts and even small snakes are all fair game in the fish world, as long as the predator's mouth is big enough.

WEATHER, SEASONS & CHANGING CONDITIONS

For most normal folk, the weather is small talk. To an angler it can make or break a fishing trip. Fish and their habitats are hugely affected by wind, rain and seasonal changes, with different species adopting distinct lifestyles. Understanding these changes is part of the challenge of angling, and in many ways we pit our wits against the weather as well as the fish.

WHAT IS THE BEST TIME TO GO FISHING?

Through every twelve-month cycle, bodies of water undergo huge changes. As cold-blooded creatures, fish are at the mercy of shifting temperatures and trends, and the risks and opportunities these bring. Using our knowledge and experience to adapt to this is all part of the challenge of angling. Suffice to say, if we only set out in 'perfect' conditions, we'd do very little fishing!

HIGH PRESSURE (BRIGHT SKIES, LITTLE CLOUD COVER)

Different fish have their own seasons and preferences. A day of heavy rain might be poor for river trout, for example, but could see catfish or carp feeding hard. Over time, we can build a picture to guide us and get the best of each month of the year. This is also where being an 'all-round' angler pays off, because if we embrace variety there's always something to catch, come rain, shine or frost.

FEELING THE PRESSURE...

There's a good reason that anglers are glued to weather forecasts. Changes not only tell us to pack a raincoat or sun hat, but also inform how we fish. Perhaps the best place to start is by looking at atmospheric pressure. This is measured in inches of mercury (inHg), or millibars (hPa), depending on where you live.

HIGH PRESSURE (generally above 1,020 hPa/30.20 inHg) means heavy air, which tends to push away cloud cover, leading to clear, sunny skies.

LOW PRESSURE (generally under 1,000 hPa/29.80 inHg) in the atmosphere tends to mean more cloud cover, often accompanied by rain and increased winds. Very low pressure can also bring storms or gales.

Pressure affects fish in different ways, but suffice to say ideal picnic weather is not always productive for fishing. Anglers even use the term 'fair-weather fisher' for someone who prefers a sun tan to a bend in the rod. This brings us to our next golden rule: successful anglers put the preferences of fish before their own! After all, our finned friends couldn't care less if we are warm, comfortable or out of the wind.

LOW PRESSURE (DULL SKIES, INCREASED CHANCE OF RAIN AND WIND)

HOW DOES THE WIND IMPACT FISHING?

Choppy water often emboldens fish by both masking our presence and stirring the water to life. You may have heard the old saying: 'when the wind is East the fish bite least/when the wind is West the fish bite best' or even 'when the wind is in the south, the fish opens its mouth.' Not the worst advice, because southerly and westerly winds tend to be warmer, while those coming from the north and east often carry a chill.

One good rule for any angler is not to avoid the wind, but to use it. If the breeze is warm, fish will generally follow it, because the wind will push food and warmer water to one side of a lake; put your comfort second and you might have a great catch! If the wind is cold, however, this can have the opposite effect, with the fish likely to favour more sheltered spots. In extreme circumstances, like a storm or gale, fish will often move in during or after the event to mop up dislodged or disoriented prey items. However, this comes with a warning…

Fish tend to feed more confidently and are more tolerant of shallower water.

The wind increases oxygen levels and stirs up food, such as fly life. A ripple on the water also makes fish less wary of humans and fishing line.

The angler can be bolder when feeding bait, and use larger and more obvious lures and flies to appeal to hungry, active fish.

A SHOCKING TALE

The carbon used for modern rods and poles is an excellent electrical conductor, hence a thunderstorm is no time to be fishing! A lake angler in southern England found this out the hard way in 2013, after receiving a huge lightning shock. He fitted so hard that the friend who came to help him had several teeth knocked out. Luckily, he survived, but every year anglers are killed by storms, as well as by power lines.

HOW DOES THE TEMPERATURE AFFECT FISHING?

As cold-blooded animals, fish have lower appetites and activity levels as the mercury drops. For the angler, this might mean fishing lures slower or introducing less bait. That's not to say very high temperatures are best, however. As with hot, muggy air, warm water contains less dissolved oxygen. Hence, just like humans, fish can be sluggish on a sultry, humid afternoon. The temperature of water can also be very different to the air. There will be warmer and cooler layers in any body of water, separated by a level or change zone known as the thermocline.

In hot, dry spells, even large fish will often head for shallow, faster water because these areas are rich in oxygen.

Fish will seek a comfortable temperature and good oxygen levels; it's up to the angler to find out which level in the water the fish prefer. This changes seasonally, and different species have their own preferences. Trout and pike, for instance, struggle in warm water, whereas carp and catfish thrive.

HOW DO RAIN & FLOODING IMPACT FISH?

Another constant factor for angling is rainfall. It's not that a shower instantly affects the fish (unlike us, they are already wet), but an influx of water can bring about major changes. After a very dry spell, for instance, a period of rain and lower air pressure can bring a fishery back to life.

On rivers, the impact of rain, or a lack of it, is especially key. Look at a stream in drought and flood, and you might barely recognise it as the same place. Heavy or prolonged rain is liable not only to make the water level rise, but also to affect the clarity. For some types of fish and fishing, such as targeting bottom feeders with bait, this might be ideal. If you are a fly fisher, however, or seek fish that feed primarily by sight, the opposite is true. By and large, fish are warier in very clear water than in murky conditions. Trial, error and experience

The clearer and shallower the water, the easier fish scare. A cautious approach and smaller, more realistic flies, lures and baits make sense.

Aside from confirmed bottom dwellers, like barbel and catfish, many fish species will head for the upper water layers on sunny days.

are the best teachers, but for every challenging scenario in angling there will also be an opportunity nearby. Some brilliant fishing can be had on waters dropping and clearing after a heavy flood, for instance. For the fish this must be like someone turning the lights back on after a long night! However you look at it, there are only two certainties in angling: when the going is bad, it will always get better at some stage. When things are great, make the most of it because bites will eventually tail off.

Above all, the angler should treat every water as a dynamic and ever-changing environment. Even a tiny stream or pond is a mystery to be solved, with lots of variables. In many ways, the times you fail to catch fish are as important as your successes. Even if you catch nothing, a fishing trip is never wasted if you've learned something. It's this delayed gratification and the process of figuring things out that makes angling so satisfying.

HIGH OR FLOODED RIVER

PATTERNS OF CHANGE & TRANSITION PERIODS

As well as aspects like sun, wind and rain on any given day, it is also helpful to look at the 'bigger picture' over several days. What patterns can we spot? In general, fish like stability. For example, while they might feel settled after a week of cool weather, a sudden overnight drop in temperature is likely to make for tough fishing.

Another obvious pattern is the sequence of night and day. Very often, anglers who rise early or stay up late enjoy better results than those who only fish convenient daytime hours. Dawn and dusk, in particular, are key times of change and activity. Night fishing can also be worthwhile, and one little discussed reason for this is so-called invertebrate drift – which refers to peak times of movement for the tiny animals fish eat. Suffice to say, changing your clock is frequently a good way to change your fishing results.

Where water clarity is poor, fish are less wary but may require a bolder, smellier or more obvious lure or bait.

Areas like snags, slacks and side streams now become important places for fish to shelter while they wait for the water level to come down. Undercut banks and submerged rocks are another classic shelter, and even large fish can sit right under the bank.

STRANGE FISHING LOCATIONS

What is the weirdest place you might catch a fish? Some of the places anglers have successfully cast a line truly defy belief! You never know until you try, however. Nor are all the interesting features on our rivers, lakes and seas strictly natural. If you can stand the stench or noise, for instance, some excellent fishing can be found everywhere from power stations and factories to abattoirs!

THE LAKES OF CHERNOBYL Nuclear disaster in Northern Ukraine in 1986 led to the abandonment of large areas of wilderness and lakes. While you might imagine mutated and deformed animals caused by the fallout, in reality wildlife thrived. TV adventurer Jeremy Wade was one of the few anglers brave enough to visit, catching a catfish that had sixteen times the normal radiation levels.

DROWNED VILLAGES AND GHOSTLY CHURCHES When valleys are flooded to create reservoirs, whole settlements are sometimes evacuated. During periods of drought, eerie features are sometimes exposed, many years later. The lost town of Llanwddyn, Wales, still occasionally emerges from Lake Vyrnwy in chronic dry spells. At England's Ladybower Reservoir, a trout fishery, cottages and a ghostly church spire are sometimes revealed.

Lake Titicaca in the Andes

THE DESERT LAKES OF LAS VEGAS You might associate Las Vegas with bright lights and casinos, but the surrounding area also has some surprisingly good bass fishing. Lake Mead is among the largest stillwaters, and was created by damming the Colorado River. With climate change and increasing water use, however, you might want to fish it sooner rather than later because it is shrinking, with water levels falling below 30% in recent years.

ALPINE FISHING WITH 'ALTITUDE' For those with a head for heights, there are some spectacular places to wet a line worldwide. Destinations such as the Swiss and Austrian Alps, including Lake Achensee, provide trout fishing with cool air and surreal, jade-green glacial meltwater. Other lofty destinations include California's Lake Crowley and New Zealand's Lake Wakatipu, while the highest navigable stillwater fishery in the world is Lake Titicaca in the Andes.

THE CANALS OF MIAMI While most of us think of canals as slightly humdrum, artificial waters, the channels of Miami are a world apart. Provided you manage to focus amid sunbathing iguanas and strutting peacocks, there are some real net-fillers present, including bass, snook and tarpon.

FISHING IN FLOODED FIELDS Right across Asia, flooded paddy fields are used to cultivate rice. All manner of fish make their way into these areas, including catfish, snakehead, tilapia and various carp.

CHAPTER THREE

MEET THE FISH

'I look for fish in any likely water I see – harbors, rivers, irrigation ditches, hotel lobby fountains.'

IAN FRAZIER

'Quite possibly this is the key to fishing: the ability to see glamour in whatever species one may fish for.'

HAROLD F. BLAISDELL

'A fish is too precious to be caught only once.'

LEE WULFF

'It has always been my private conviction that any man who puts his intelligence up against a fish and loses had it coming.'

JOHN STEINBECK

Making their home in such a different world to our own, fish are creatures that are both comfortingly familiar and yet mysterious to the angler. Whether it is their brilliant, glistening scales or beguiling habits, fish charm and frustrate us in equal measure. There is always another secret to uncover and, in many ways, fish are less predictable than our animal cousins on land. One obvious difference is their great variation in scale. Most mammal and bird species, for instance, grow to a similar size. You don't find one field mouse the size of a bee and another the size of a house brick. Yet with fish, there is immense difference, and the dream of finding an absolute giant is one of the great charms of angling. The same is true of the colours, patterns and habits of fish. Even the same species can be phenomenally varied between different waters. While all anglers prize fish, however, our understanding of them all too often takes a backseat to more obvious concerns like rods, lures and bait. Hence, in this chapter, we'll take a closer look at fish in all their glory, from iconic 'box office' species to genuine oddballs.

Every angler wants to catch more fish, of course, but this is not the only benefit of broadening our understanding. The more knowledge we gain about these amazing creatures and their habitats, the greater our power to protect them. Big or small, we love them all, and without fish there is no fishing.

WHAT IS A FISH?

The term 'fish' encompasses everything from deep-sea monsters to sticklebacks. Our main definition is simply animals with backbones, fins and gills, adapted to live solely in water. The category is so vast that some ecologists have debated if there even is such a thing as a fish. However, we know that fish-like animals first appeared around 530 million years ago, and that all land vertebrates, including humans, evolved from them.

- There are over 33,000 species of fish, and counting. That's more than all mammals, birds, reptiles and amphibians combined, and around 60 percent of all vertebrates. We can split the vast majority of fish into two main types, excluding very primitive jawless species:

  Teleosts, or so-called 'bony fishes', including perch, tuna and wrasse, which have light, flexible skeletons of bone.
  Cartilaginous fishes, such as sharks, rays and skates, which have skeletons made of cartilage rather than bone.
- There are 84 orders of fish. Key groups for anglers include *Salmonidae* (trout and salmon), *Perciformes* (bass, perch) and *Cypriniformes* (carp, barbel, chub and minnows).
- Besides huge differences between groups, even fish of the same species can vary greatly. Brown trout, for instance, are all *Salmo trutta*, but individuals from rivers just a few kilometres apart can be genetically very different in size and appearance.
- Some freshwater fish are labelled game species (trout and salmonids, chiefly), with the rest known as coarse or rough fish. This is because during spawning, the males of chub, dace and other species develop fine bumps or tubercles, making them rough to the touch.

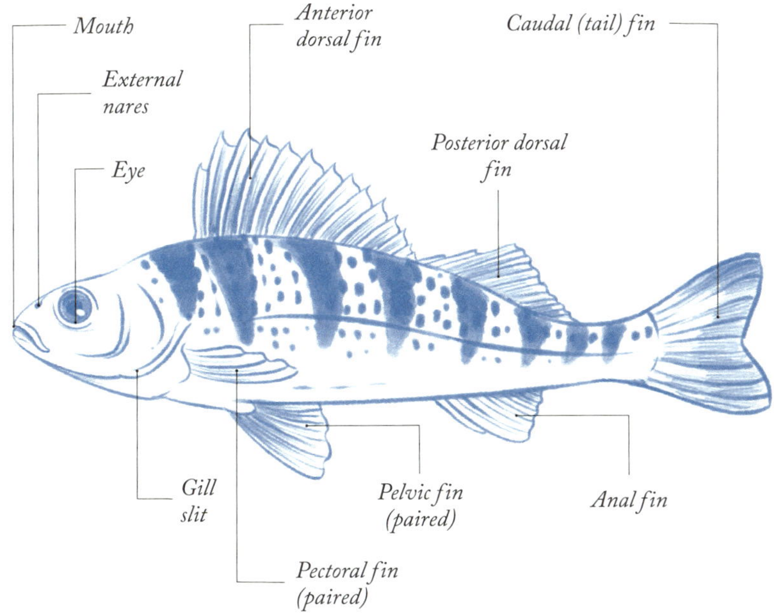

Dorsal fin or fins Can be soft or spiky; used for display or protection

Eye Size and position tell us about the fish's lifestyle

Mouth Only some fish have teeth in the mouth; many others have throat or pharyngeal teeth.

Lateral line Helps detect movement and vibration

Pectoral and pelvic fins For balance and manoeuvring

Tail and anal fin Give a fish power and forward propulsion

WHY ARE FISH SLIMY?

Most fish are covered in a layer of mucus. This protects them against infection and parasites, besides aiding swimming efficiency. It's always best to handle fish with wet hands, to avoid removing this.

SHAPES & KEY FEATURES

The forms of fish tell us a great deal about their lifestyles. Their designs have evolved over tens of millions of years, with the most effective shapes and features enduring. The basic shark blueprint, for instance, easily predates the dinosaurs.

BODY SHAPES OF FISH

Arrow or spear-shaped fish are built for speed and reduced drag. Out-and-out predators such as barracuda (*Sphyraena barracuda*), above, and needlefish are great examples.

Oval or diamond shaped profiles give a balance of speed and manoeuvrability, often denoting 'all-rounders' and omnivores, like this ide (*Leuciscus idus*).

Flat-bottomed or low-profiled fish, such as channel catfish *(Ictalarus punctatus),* are designed to lurk on the bottom or even blend in with it.

MOUTH AND HEAD SHAPES

An **overslung or downward-pointing mouth** shows that the fish is primarily a bottom feeder. It may also have whiskers or barbules for detecting food in mud, sand or debris.

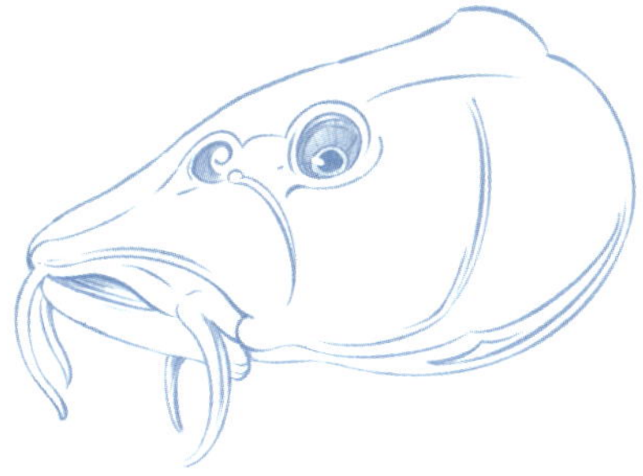

Lips of similar length often betray an adaptable fish that will feed on a variety of food at all levels.

An **upward-facing mouth or exaggerated bottom lip** suggests a fish designed to take food from below, feeding in mid-water and above. The Atlantic tarpon (*Megalops atlanticus*) is a classic example.

DO FISH REALLY 'BITE'?

While we say fish 'bite' our bait or lure, that's not necessarily the case. 'Inhale' is usually more accurate. When the mouth opens, a vacuum is created, sucking in anything directly in front of it. For a larger specimen, this can seem quite effortless, and is perhaps why we only get a gentle initial pluck on the line when a fish first 'bites'. The rod thumping over or line pulling away is the fish already moving off with dinner.

Fish don't tend to chew food like humans. Most swallow it whole. The sharp teeth of predators are mainly to stop prey escaping, although some fish have crushing teeth to tackle tough meals, like shellfish. Other fish use pharyngeal teeth in their throats, which would be a bit like you chewing a steak you've already swallowed.

Many fish suck in food and blow it out as if testing it, which is why we often get little taps and nibbles as well as more obvious pulls. Lots of species take in mouthfuls of sand, mud or organic matter as they feed, holding onto the good bits and blowing out the rest.

SPECIAL FEATURES, SIGNALS AND DETERRENTS

The fish world is litterd with special features and adaptations. Gurnards, or 'sea robins', not only swim, but also crawl along the ocean floor using specially adapted, limb-like fins. Peacock bass are one of several species displaying a 'false eye' on the tail, thought to be a way to confuse predators.

COLORATION IN FISH

Many fish have scales that are silver, bronze or gold thanks to guanine, a light-reflective crystalline substance that makes them harder to spot. Ironically, it's perhaps this shimmer that makes humans see fish as living treasure. In the case of bleak, a small and silvery fish, this is literally true because the scales were once used to make artificial pearls.

From above: Grey, green or bluish hues help fish avoid detection from predators such as birds and humans.

From below: Many fish species are pale or whitish, to blend with the light of the sky from the perspective of predators lurking below.

Other fish have different ways to avoid detection, whether that is lying flush to the sand in the case of flatfish, or using spots, stripes and other patterning. Many can also change colour.

In locations such as tropical seas, however, other fish take the opposite approach and use bright colours to stand out a mile. This can be to signal to shoalmates, to emphasise their own space on a busy coral reef, or even to warn predators of toxicity.

THE LIFE CYCLES OF FISH

It is startling to think that even the fish of a lifetime started out smaller than a sunflower seed. Breeding habits and lifespans are spectacularly varied in fish.

- Most of the biggest fish are female – which makes sense, because the bigger mama is, the more eggs she can lay. It's also why you should always release the biggest fish.
- Survival by numbers is the usual strategy for fish. The odds of making it to adulthood are slim, especially if you are one of the 300 million eggs a single ocean sunfish can lay!
- But not all fish are lousy parents. An alternative strategy is to have fewer young but defend them. Some fish, including sticklebacks and cichlids, make nests.

As tiny as sticklebacks are, they are ferociously protective nest builders.

Greenland sharks can live for 400 years.

LIFESPANS AND GROWTH RATES

The growth rates and metabolism of fish run to great extremes, and size does not always indicate young or old age. In a cold, nutrient-poor lake, for instance, a 6in (15cm) trout might be a decade old. Maturity also varies. Fish like cod and perch breed like rabbits. Large, slow-growing fish can take years to reproduce, however, which makes them more vulnerable to exploitation.

The potential age and size of any fish is dependent on many factors, including food, water quality and competition. Anglers get obsessed with weight and length, but in truth all measurements are relative. A 1lb (0.45kg) fish might be small in a stocked lake, but a giant in a tiny stream. It's good reason to set your own bar and ignore social media!

LONG-LIVED FISH
Greenland sharks: 400 years+
Rougheye rockfish: 200+ years
Longfin eel: 100+ years

SHORT-LIVED FISH
Pygmy goby: maximum 59 days
African turquoise killifish: 4–6 months
Common minnow: 2–4 years

FISH SENSES

Thanks to modern science, we now understand just how complex and well-adapted fish are. But how sharp are their senses and how does this inform angling? Can fish see and hear us? And can we ever consider them as intelligent?

FISH EYESIGHT

The eyesight of fish varies greatly, but our first clue is to look at the size and position of the eyes. A catfish in a muddy pond is vastly different to a trout in a crystal-clear river. Fish living at great depths, such as Atlantic cod, have huge eyes, while others have tiny, nearly useless eyes. Just like land animals, the position of eyes on a fish reflect its lifestyle. For omnivorous shoal fish (L) such as a roach or bream, eyes on the sides of the head give all-round vision to detect shoal mates and potential danger. On a predator (R) however, the eyes are higher on the head and forward facing, to provide binocular vision. Species like pike and snook even have grooves on their skulls like rifle sights.

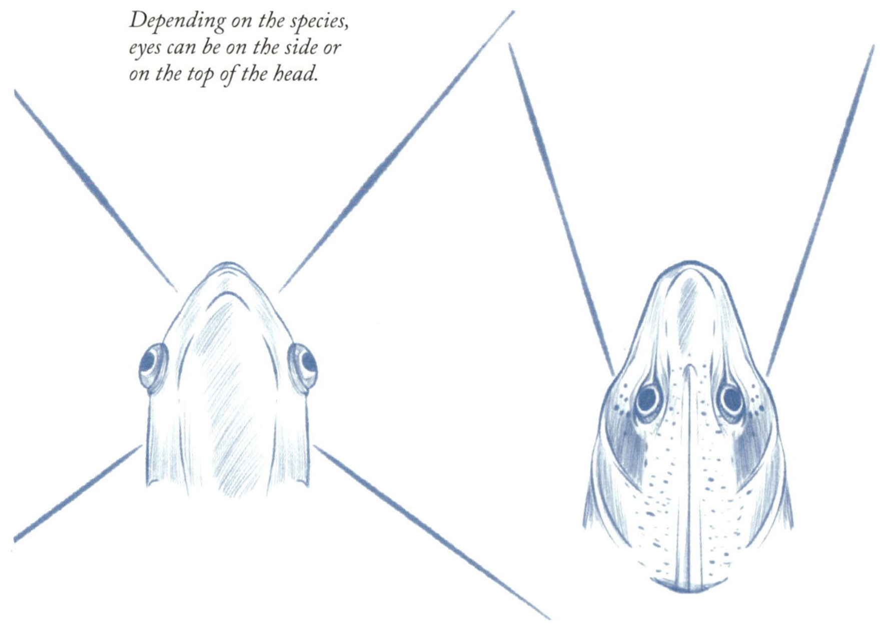

Depending on the species, eyes can be on the side or on the top of the head.

A stealthy angler uses cover to mask their presence, and will crouch or kneel to keep off the skyline, especially at close range or with keen-sighted fish.

CAN FISH SEE US?

In many cases, fish are wary of anglers, especially in clear or shallow water, and in still or sunny conditions. Smart anglers are never complacent and we probably scare more fish than we ever realise. As aquarium owners will know, calm waters create a mirror effect, allowing fish to see friends and foes reflected when they look up.

WAYS TO AVOID SCARING FISH

- Move slowly and carefully.
- Wear drab clothing and watch your shadow on bright days.
- When fishing close to the bank, keep a sensible distance back, crouch down and use any cover available.
- On fast-flowing rivers, cast from a downstream position if possible; most fish face into the current.
- Think about your tackle, including the thickness of lines and the size of hooks, lures and flies. The shallower and clearer the water, the warier the fish.

FISH HEARING AND VIBRATION DETECTION

Sound travels five times faster in water than air, and while fish lack external ears like ours, they have internal hearing chambers. These contain fine hairs or bony growths, and are usually behind the eyes. Fish can hear rushing currents, stones knocking, and very possibly even a worm wriggling nearby. Researchers have even found that some fish communicate with clicks, croaks and grunts.

Closely linked to these abilities is the capacity to detect vibration. Fish can sense movement through their lateral line, while tiny pores in the body and the swim bladder also pick up on wave patterns. They can clearly detect currents, friends, foes and even tiny pressure changes. Some fish manage to hunt in pitch-black conditions, while others, such as cavefish, lack eyes and are completely blind. Species like rays and sharks can detect electrical impulses, but that's another plug-in kettle of fish altogether!

No sight is no problem for the eyeless cavefish.

Key angling takeaways on sound and vibration detection in fish

- When bank fishing, most sound will be reflected off the water's surface. We're probably OK to talk, but should avoid shouting or stomping about.
- When transmitted via a solid object (i.e. the bottom of a boat or rocks we're wading over), sound travels very efficiently. In these scenarios, take extra care.
- When casting, it usually pays to make our sinker, lure or fly land as gently as possible to avoid alarming the fish. However, on occasion a splash can be attractive, such as when a predator expects crashing, fleeing prey.
- In murky water or where fish can see little, we might boost our chances by picking lures and flies that create extra vibration.

WHAT DO FISH SMELL AND TASTE?

Just as we can instantly smell fried chicken or a pile of garbage, fish are sensitive to scent and taste. These two things tend to blur together in water, which can carry smells a long way, and some fish are incredibly sensitive. Carp, for instance, can detect one drop of flavour in an Olympic-size swimming pool. Sharks can smell thousands of times better than us, picking up a scent trail from miles away.

Things get even stranger with taste organs. Fish do not smell through nostrils, as we do, but have well-developed taste buds. These are not always limited to mouths and throats, but can be on the snout, whiskers, and even the fins and tail in the case of catfish, which would be like you tasting breakfast by sitting on it!

Capitalising on smell and taste

- For scent-feeding fish or waters with poor visibility, strong-smelling baits make sense.
- Consider building a scent trail by ground baiting or chumming, or cutting open oily fish baits, especially for species like sharks and catfish.
- Avoid contaminating your bait and rigs with human smells, like soap or cleaning products. Some anglers won't stop to refuel their vehicle on a fishing trip!
- Experiment with flavourings and scents. Most fish like salt, while some like sweet, spicy or savoury flavours.

HOW CLEVER ARE FISH?

Are fish truly capable of 'thinking'? Fish typically have brains one-fifteenth the size of birds or mammals, but this doesn't mean they lack sophisticated survival instincts and behaviours. Fish display 'learned behaviour', whether that means avoiding a busy corner of the lake or rejecting suspicious baits and lures. In fact, various scientific studies back up the old saying 'once bitten, twice shy', with fish clearly becoming harder to catch after encountering hooks. Here are some useful lessons:

- **Never assume that fish are stupid.** All have strong survival instincts and may be suspicious of humans and fishing tackle.
- **Larger and longer-lived fish tend to be the smartest,** because they've built up more experience and nature favours the shrewd. Large carp, for example, can evade capture for years on end, even on heavily fished lakes.
- **Loners are usually smarter than shoaling fish** for similar reasons. In many species, solitary fish are big and wily, unlike their smaller, younger cousins that are competing with each other. It's a curious fact of angling that big fish often bite more gently than little ones.
- **Fishing pressure always tends to make fish wary,** as they learn to avoid certain locations and danger signals. Smart anglers respond by changing spots, times, baits or tactics.

CULT FISH SPECIES

TROUT

Sharpsighted and adept at rising for their food, which includes various invertebrates as well as small fish, trout are also perfectly suited to perhaps angling's all-time cult method: fly fishing. Mankind's love of trout is responsible for its spread all over the globe. In the days of the British Empire, homesick anglers introduced brown trout everywhere from the lakes of Massachusetts to the rivers of New Zealand. In return, European settlers in America quickly fell in love with the new varieties they found, spreading the rainbow trout and its relatives far beyond their natural range.

Aside from their broad appetite and the way they leap when hooked, another reason we love trout is their stunning variety. Mountain trout are different to lowland trout; some fish are spattered with hundreds of tiny spots, while others have just a few big polka dots. Even on the same river, each trout is as unique as a fingerprint.

The rainbow trout: a beautiful, bold fighter.

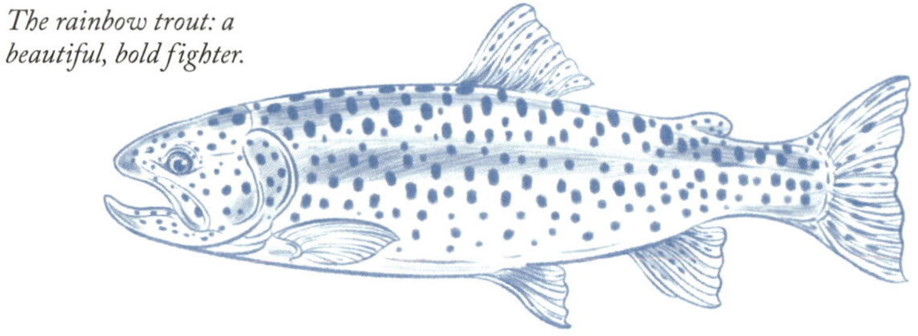

- The brown trout (*Salmo trutta*) is native to Europe, while the rainbow trout (*Oncorhynchus mykiss*) is native to the USA, Mexico and Canada. Others include the cutthroat trout (*Oncorhynchus clarkii*), named after the bold red 'cut' on its lower jaw, and Europe's beautiful marbled trout (*Salmo marmoratus*).
- Some trout migrate to sea, which allows females to grow larger and lay more eggs. Ocean-going browns are called sea trout, while rainbows are known as steelhead.
- Trout have been introduced to every continent except Antarctica.

The sea bass epitomises the big mouth, spiky dorsal fin and powerful frame of the family.

BASS

Found in various guises worldwide, bass species have a phenomenally successful shared blueprint: a powerful, solid frame, along with a spiky dorsal fin and a big mouth not to be messed with. Supremely adaptable, they are the SUV of the fish world, seemingly able to travel anywhere and eat almost anything, whether it's a frog, a crawdad or smaller fish. Technically, we can split the most popular angling species into separate clans: in freshwater, we have the black basses of the *Micropterus* or sunfish family. The real showstoppers are the largemouth bass (*Micropterus nigricans*) and smallmouth bass (*Micropterus dolomieu*). Beautiful, aggressive and fascinating, no other fish in history has spawned such a vast array of fishing lures, and in the USA, bass fishing is a huge industry loved by Sunday anglers and professionals alike.

Sharing a similar blueprint of tough, spiky frame and big mouth in saltwater is the related *Moronidae* family, which includes European seabass (*Dicentrarchus labrax*) and the similar-looking striped bass (*Morone saxatilis*). Just like their freshwater counterparts, they are voracious, versatile predators that can be tempted with bait, lures or even fly tackle.

- The name 'bass' originates from the Middle English word 'bars', which means 'perch'.
- Freshwater bass have been too successful in some cases. In parts of Japan and Spain, for instance, they are now regarded as invasive, outcompeting (or simply eating) native species.
- Part of the success of freshwater bass is down to smart parenting. Many species make nests, which they defend. A female largemouth carries 4,000 eggs per pound of weight, and to get a broader mix of genes she sheds eggs in clusters, which are fertilised by different males.
- Other popular strains include spotted bass, white bass, peacock bass and Japanese sea bass.

PIKE

Among the world's legendary freshwater predators, the very name 'pike' comes from the old English word 'pik' – meaning spear or point. It's not just the size and acute predatory instincts that anglers love, but the eerie sense of encountering a prehistoric monster. A design classic, the pike has changed little in 50 million years, as fossils confirm.

Built for speed rather than stamina, pike are a thrilling sport fish. Their blink-and-you'll-miss-it savagery is the stuff of legend. Stories of leviathans and drowned mules are hogwash, but pike have occasionally grabbed small dogs, and are also partial to water birds and even their own siblings. Indeed, similar-sized pike have occasionally been found locked together in a death grip.

Although most at home in cool, northerly waters, pike have a surprisingly wide range, further increased by anglers. They can be caught by bait, lure or even fly fishing, and continue to inspire wild tales. In spite of the bad rep, however, pike play a key part in freshwater ecosystems. Hence, the days of demonising this fantastic predator are largely gone.

The northern pike is a beguiling assassin of ancient origins.

- The most common fish in the family is the northern pike (*Esox lucius*). The chain pickerel (*Esox niger*) is its miniature cousin, while the mightiest of the clan is the Muskelunge or Muskie (*Esox masquinongy*).
- Large pike are always female and can be over a yard long, dwarfing the males. A big female can lay over half a million eggs.
- Pike have up to 700 pin-sharp teeth. These are used to prevent prey escaping rather than for tearing or chewing.
- In spite of its mean looks, pike are fragile and it's vital to handle them with respect. They should be left alone in warm conditions – and novices should find a guide or experienced angler to assist them.

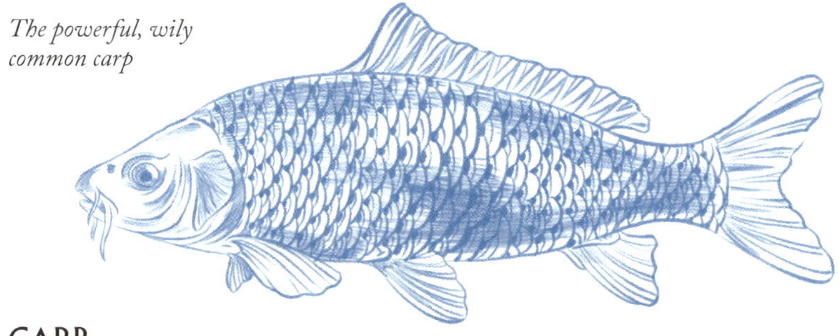
The powerful, wily common carp

CARP

Large, long-lived and adaptable, the carp has found its way to almost every corner of the globe. Perhaps no fish in history has been worshipped and reviled to the same extent. In Europe, giant, elusive fish are coveted and even given names by angling obsessives. In other countries, they are regarded as an invasive menace, to be targeted with poison and even explosives.

From a purely angling perspective, however, carp have a lot going for them. They're handsome, grow big and have incredible power and stamina. As a long-lived species, they can also become supremely wily and challenging. Furthermore, their natural hardiness makes them ideal for busy fisheries, since they can easily survive being caught and released many times.

While there are various carp worldwide, angling is predominantly for common and mirror carp. Both are technically *Cyprinus carpio*, but while 'commons' are evenly covered in smaller scales, mirror carp were originally bred for eating, their large and sparse scales rendering them easier to prepare. Much of their early spread was by monasteries for food, but these days carp farming is worth huge sums of money, with angling at the centre of trade.

- Carp have an excellent sense of smell and are also sensitive to vibrations. They seem to like sweet and salty baits, but are intolerant of noisy or careless anglers.
- Carp are hardy and tolerant of warm, oxygen-depleted water. In some European countries, they are still kept for Christmas dinner, surviving for a few days in the family bathtub.
- Koi Carp (*Cyprinus rubrofuscus*) are highly prized and can live even longer than other carp, occasionally to over 100. A fish named 'S Legend' sold for US $1.8 million (£1.3 million) in 2018!

INCREDIBLE SPECIES WORLDWIDE

ATLANTIC SALMON

An iconic species from the Scottish Highlands to Canada, these fish possess stunning bright silver scales and incredible athleticism. With uncanny homing instincts, their journeys can span thousands of miles.

BONEFISH

Nicknamed the 'ghost of the flats', these creatures are not only hard to spot due to their flawless camouflage, but challenging to tempt. The game is not even over when you hook one, because they can shift at the sort of pace that would make an Olympic sprinter jealous, hitting 40mph (about 65km/h)!

TIGERFISH

Quite literally armed to the teeth, these African predators are the stuff of legend. The family includes several members, including the fearsome goliath tigerfish that reaches over 100lb (45kg).

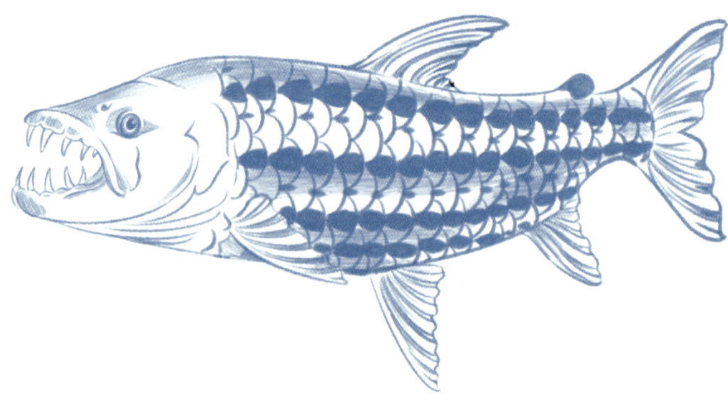

MAHSEER

India's legendary gamefish has attracted angling pilgrims for many years. A versatile, powerful river dweller, it's famed for its awe-inspiring strength and beauty.

TARPON

For many saltwater anglers, the tarpon is the ultimate game fish. With spectacular armoured scales, it is famed for its searing power and heart-stopping leaps.

MARLIN AND BILLFISH

The so-called billfish family (they have long, bony snouts or beaks, that give them quite a spectacular appearance) represent one of the most breathtaking angling challenges on the planet. The daddy of them all is the black marlin, which can weigh over 1000lb (450kg), while the sailfish is the fastest fish on earth, hitting speeds of 68mph (about 100km/h).

TUNA

Imagine watching an area the size of a football field erupting with baitfish, followed by a hooked fish that takes 200yd (about 180m) of line before even slowing down, and you have the thrill of tuna fishing. Varieties range from the small but powerful bonito to the giant bluefin.

STURGEON

These prehistoric monsters are the world's largest freshwater fish. Now threatened in many of their former strongholds, anglers are fighting to give them better protection. The largest is Russia's beluga sturgeon, while Canada's white sturgeon are the fish of a lifetime for many visiting anglers.

FISH HANDLING & CONSERVATION

It may seem strange to an outsider, but nobody values fish more highly than the angler. And while our hobby involves hooking them, it also involves a duty of care. It is anglers who spend significant amounts of money protecting habitats and restoring rivers and raising the alarm when fish are at threat.

For an increasing number of anglers, catch and release is now the norm, either by choice or by law. Regardless of our own preferences, there are only two options when we catch a fish: we either dispatch it quickly and humanely or we return it with great care.

Golden rules for catch and release fishing

- Always follow the rules and think about sustainability. If you're not going to eat or use a fish, put it back.
- Consider using barbless hooks, or crushing down existing barbs on hooks.
- Always handle fish with wet hands and keep them out of water as little as possible.

A fish is gently held in the water to recover. The majority of fish can be released unharmed if we are careful.

- Lower fish back rather than throwing them. If a fish fights hard, hold it upright in the water and allow it time to recover.
- Have your unhooking tools and essentials ready at all times.
- Never stand or walk with a big fish! Always kneel with it, preferably over the water or something soft.
- Avoid crude, knotted nets. Modern soft mesh or rubber meshed nets are far kinder.
- Regardless of laws, always consider releasing the largest fish. These are 'spawners' that will pass on their big fish genes.

Golden rules for catch and kill

- Carry a suitable tool, such as a 'trout priest', which is a small club.
- The quickest way to kill a fish is with two or three sharp strikes on the back of the head, between the eyes.
- Be prepared with a cool bag or box. Freezing some bottles of water overnight is an easy way to create a cool space.
- Carry a sharp knife, and clean and gut your fish as soon as you can. It's sensible to cut the throat of a dispatched fish and remove the guts promptly (and you then have less mess to take home).
- In general, fileting is for larger fish, whereas smaller samples are best off cooked whole.
- Fish is always best as fresh as possible, but if you intend to freeze them, do so right away and always mark the date.

FISH PHOTOGRAPHY

Always have your camera and measuring gear ready. If you need to set up a picture, you could briefly retain your fish in a submerged landing net. The safest way to take a picture is with your fish wet and resting on a wet net. If you must have a 'grip and grin' shot, keep it brief and cradle your catch rather than squeezing it.

Always think about the background and angle of the sun. Fish colours look best facing into the light. Frame your picture with care and avoid needless empty spaces. You want the fish to be the star, but many phones and cameras will auto focus on human faces, so beware! A good way to check is to make sure the eye of the fish is in sharp focus.

CHAPTER FOUR

FISHING CRAFTS & COOKING

'He who ties his own flies and makes his own rods and tackle will have a keener personal interest in his pastime.'
LEROY MILTON

'Fishing has never lent itself to the kind of satisfaction on demand that technology has trained us to expect.'
JOHN GIERACH

'There have been far more fish caught on a hunk of yarn than on the fanciest fly ever tied.'
R. HAIG-BROWN

'If people concentrated on the really important things in life, there'd be a shortage of fishing poles.'
DOUG LARSON

One of the greatest joys of angling is the satisfaction of using your own brains and handiwork. We might live in an age when virtually anything and everything can be obtained at the touch of a screen, but this can be a curse as well as a blessing. We gain so much from angling crafts, whether it's making our own unique tackle or getting the best from freshly caught fish.

Angling is, after all, not just a pastime that puts us firmly in the present moment, but one that allows us to connect with the skills and creativity of our ancestors. And while we are always free to walk into a giant outdoor retailer and grab items off the shelf, what fun is any activity if everything is done for us?

On that basis, perhaps it's time we sparked a revival for homemade fishing tackle. Today, a whole new generation is discovering the joy of making, cooking and crafting. Technology can be a friend rather than a foe here. There might be ten million lures and flies on sale across the Internet, but we can also find countless materials, tips and tutorials to make our own.

This section of the book is an invitation to explore and enjoy some gateway skills. Get a taste for 'rolling your own' and you never know where the journey might lead. You're unlikely to save much money, let alone time, by fashioning your own lures or even building a rod, but that feeling of catching fish using something you made is priceless. Similarly, fish always tastes better when you caught it yourself!

MAKE A SIMPLE FISHING FLY

Fly tying is a fascinating hobby in its own right. Virtually all insects and prey items can be copied and it's rewarding in more ways than one. While it can take years to master fly tying, simple and deadly patterns can quite quickly be learned. A 'soft hackle' fly (aka 'spider') is an excellent example of this. Beyond a vice, scissors and a bobbin holder, all you need is a hook (size 12–16, typically), black thread, silver wire and a black hen feather. Of course, you can try various other materials and colours, and this style of fly works for coarse and pan fish besides trout.

BLACK & SILVER SPIDER

1 Fasten a hook in your vice. Pinch the end of your thread against the shank, just behind the eye, and wrap it with a few tight turns – until it 'catches' firm. Now go down the hook in touching turns, so you have a neat, thread-covered shank. Stop just above the barb.

2 Now add a piece of silver wire on top of the hook shank. Trap it in place with touching wraps of thread to secure it, working the back towards the eye.

3 Now twist the wire round the hook, making firm, even turns to create our 'rib'. Secure in place with tight wraps of thread once you reach ⅛in (2–3mm) from the eye and trim off. You needn't use scissors, just 'worry' the silver wire by wiggling from side to side until it snaps off neatly.

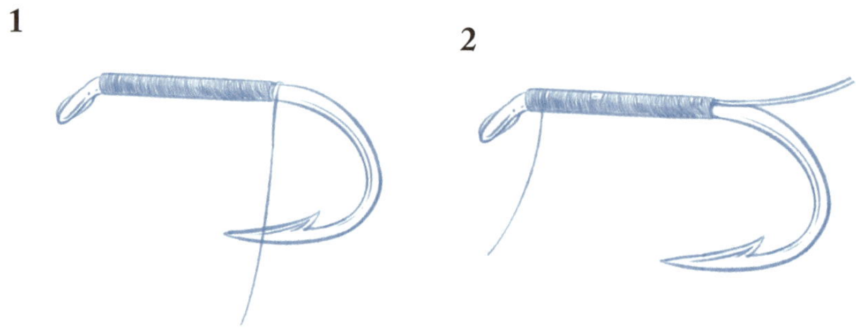

4 Pick a hen feather for your 'hackle'. Keep this in proportion (the fibres should be about half to two-thirds the length of the hook). Gently stroke out the fibres between your fingers to prepare, before tying in just behind the hook eye with 2–3 tight thread wraps.

5 Carefully wind the feather 3–4 times around the hook to create your 'hackle'. You can do this with your fingertips, but 'hackle pliers' make the job less fiddly. Now secure in place with a couple of tight wraps of thread, and snip off the excess feather. To finish, most fly tyers use a simple overhand knot or a 'whip finish' tool, but if you're a beginner, you could simply apply a spot of varnish or superglue to the thread at the front, then cut once it is dry.

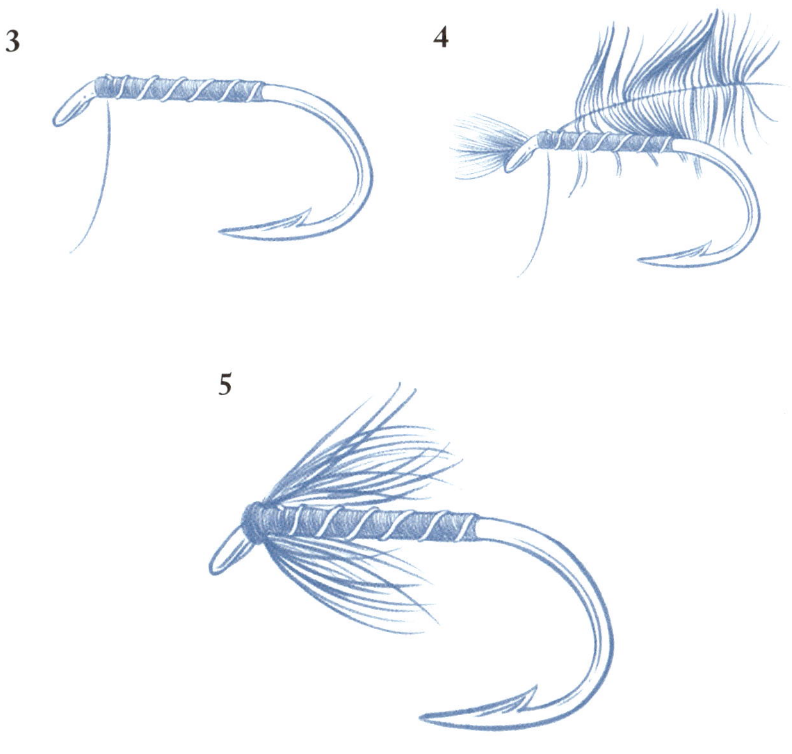

HOW TO MAKE BASIC FISHING LURES

It's only relatively recently that anglers have had access to thousands of lures at a click. This might save us hassle, but it also means we risk missing out on the enjoyment earlier generations had. Making your own lures is immensely satisfying. It's easy to get started, and you can begin with simple, everyday materials. To take just one example, where did you think we got the term 'spoon' for a basic metal lure?

1. Get a suitable-sized, silver-coloured spoon, and saw off the end.
2. Using a file or disc sander, smooth down any sharp edges. Use eye protection and gloves with any power tools.
3. Use a drill to make a hole at each end of the spoon.
4. Add a split ring to each hole, and fasten a hook at one end and a swivel at the other.

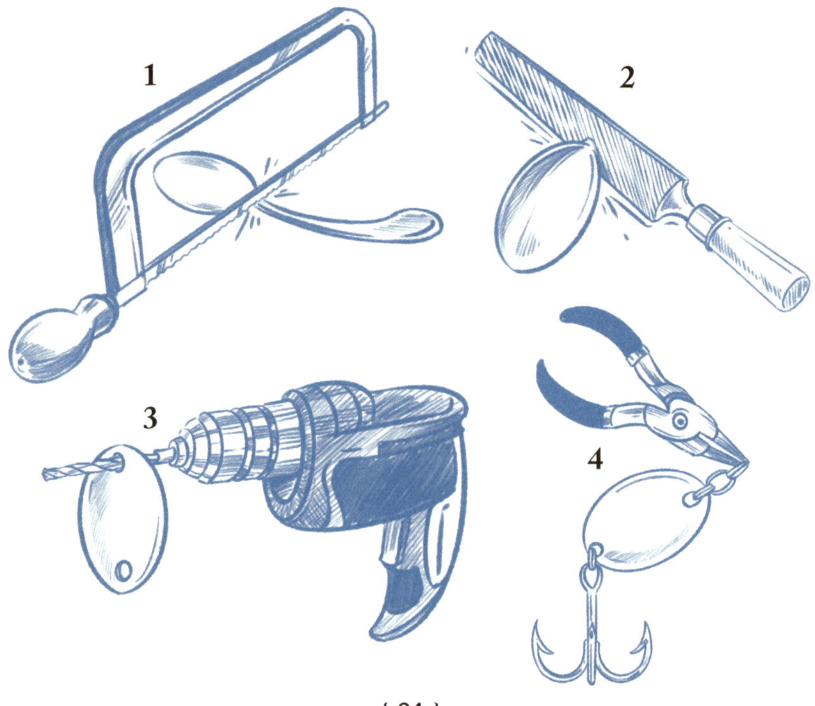

FURTHER LURE IDEAS

- Hooks can be 'dressed' with feathers and tinsel for extra attraction. This is also a good way to enhance shop-bought lures.
- You could also try staining, painting or adding an eye.
- Experiment with different shapes by filing your lure into a slimmer profile, or hammering to produce a shallower curve.

MAKING SIMPLE WOODEN LURES

Another accessible way to create your own lures is by whittling balsa or other woods into different shapes. You can start with just a tubular piece of wood, a craft knife and glass paper.

A wide, concave face can be used to make a surface popper, or try a more pointed head, before gluing in a plastic vane to create a diving crank bait.

The key is to try and get such lures as symmetrical as you can. You'll also want to cut a slot in the belly, into which you can insert some weight (such as split shot) for balance, plus a length of wire to attach hooks securely. Add hooks, paint and varnish and you have a classic fish catcher!

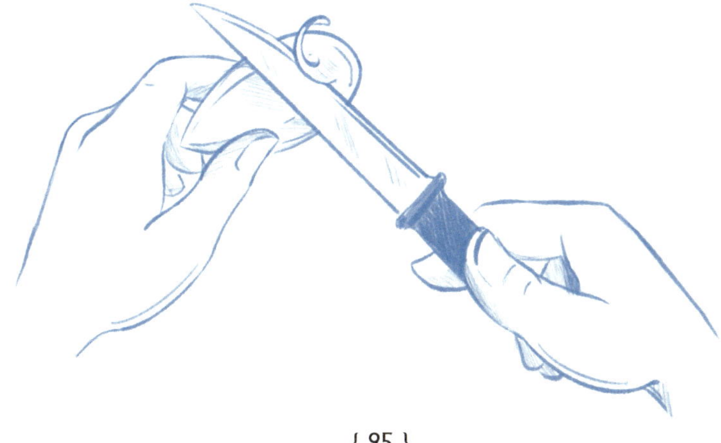

HOW TO PREPARE & COOK FISH

Where it is permitted and sustainable, keeping a fish or two for the table is one of angling's bonuses. Whether it's a cod or a rainbow trout, the golden rules are the same: process it promptly, store with care and eat as fresh as possible! Anyone can learn to clean, gut and cook fish – but time spent watching an expert is never wasted.

CLEANING AND SCALING FISH

Regardless of how you want to eat your fish, basic preparation starts with cleaning your fish in fresh water. Some species have larger scales that you'll want to remove; others are easier. One good tip for slimy specimens is to roll them in newspaper when cleaning, as the slime sticks to this.

Scaling is easiest with a whole fish, prior to any filleting or other prep. Hold by the tail or under the gills, preferably with a glove, and 'stroke' against the grain with an old knife or fish scaler tool.

HOW TO CLEAN AND GUT A FISH

Taking the guts from a fish is a messy but essential job. Doing this job outdoors is recommended, so you can prevent stinking out your kitchen and can reuse any waste by tossing it for the birds or other fish. If you lack this option, dispose of waste with care, and wrap it well if it's going in the family rubbish bin.

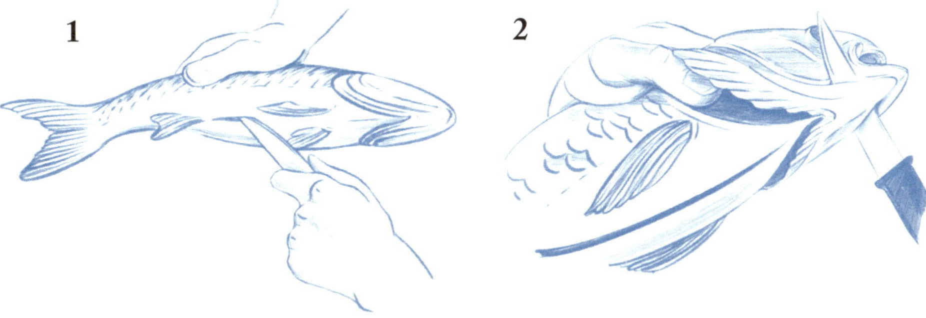

1. Insert the point of a sharp knife into the anal vent of the fish, and cut a long line up to the throat.
2. Cut through the throat and gullet to separate these from the head.
3. Holding the fish by the jaw, pull out the guts.
4. Take the blade of a knife or flat-edged tool and scrape out any further mess. Many fish have their liver attached to the backbone, visible as a dark mass. Finally, wash out the body cavity with clean water.

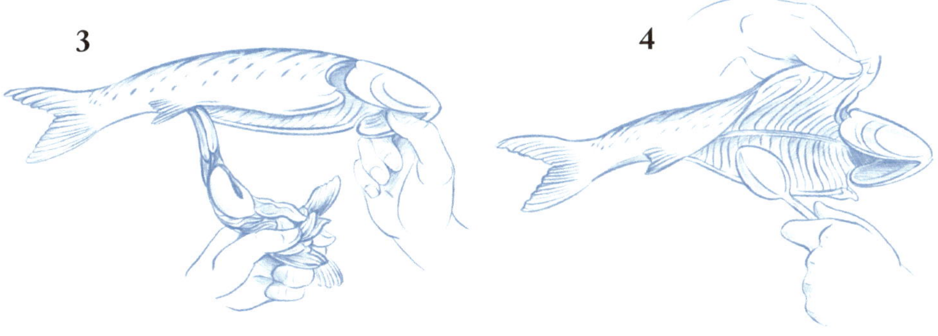

FILETING AND BONING FISH

Fileting tends to be best with larger and less bony fish. With smaller samples, it's often easier to clean, gut and cook them whole.

1 With a sharp knife, cut in just behind the gills and stop when you feel the spine.

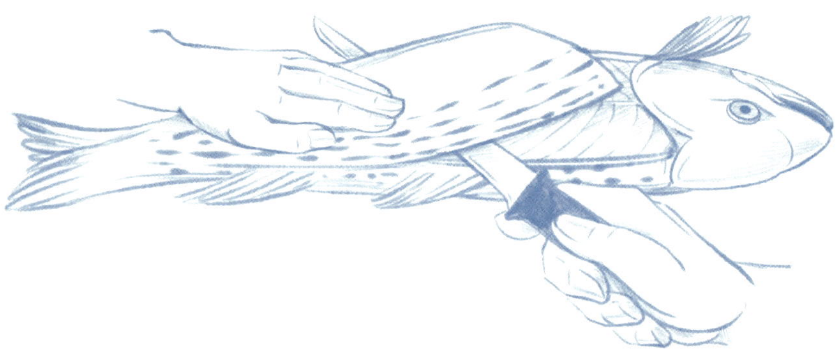

2 Now turn the knife and run it along the backbone, right to the tail.

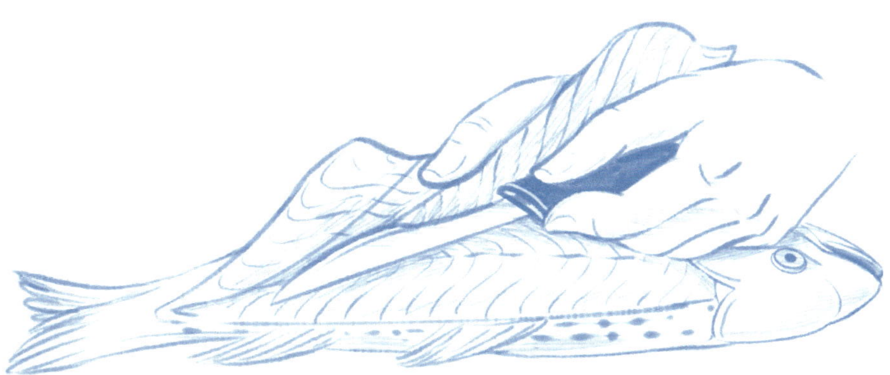

3 Lay your fillet skin-down and find the ribs, which run along the lower half. Run the knife carefully under and along these, before discarding them.

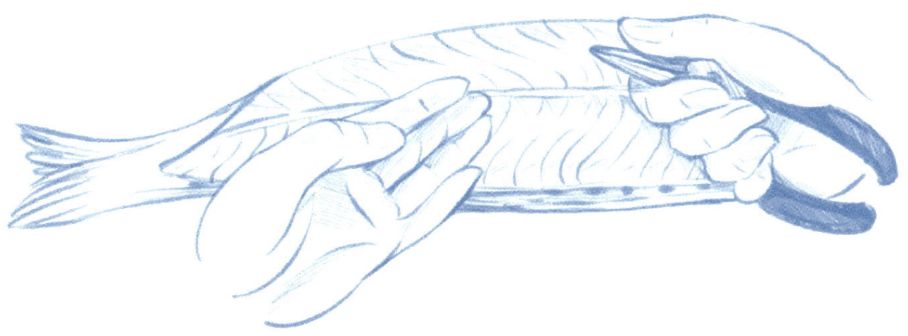

4 Run the back of your knife along the fillet to locate any stray bones, which can then be plucked out. Fine pliers or forceps are handy for this job.

BAKING FISH WHOLE

This is the easiest cooking method of all. This retains fat and flavour and saves a lot of fuss. Once well cooked, the meat can be pulled straight off the bone.

- Once you've cleaned and gutted your fish, brush inside and out with some oil or butter, along with salt, pepper and any other seasoning.

- You can also marinade or stuff a fish for baking. Garlic, herbs and lemon are all good choices to add to the body cavity.
- Adding some cuts to the skin can help you work in salt and spices. You can then wrap the fish in foil to retain flavour and moisture.
- Put your fish on a baking sheet in a preheated oven at 180°C/360°F and allow approximately 10 minutes for every inch (2.5cm) of thickness.
- You can also BBQ or grill fish in a similar manner, wrapped in foil. Expect cooking times to be faster.

FRYING FISH

This is ideal for fillets or whole smaller fish. It's quick and tasty, and if the fish is extra fresh, simple is often best.

- Prepare your fish by adding some salt, pepper and spices. If you're keeping the skin on, make some slits to work in flavour and prevent curling.
- An alternative is to brush with beaten egg, before dipping in flour or breadcrumbs – perfect for white fish like cod, perch or zander/walleye.
- Add some butter or vegetable oil to a hot pan, before adding your fish. Cooking time will depend on thickness but 3–4 minutes per side is typical (don't forget to flip over) or until golden brown.

FURTHER FISH COOKING TIPS AND IDEAS

- **Yes, you can eat fish skin!** This is down to personal preference and species. Some fish have delicious, fatty skin, others are less appetising.
- **Easy marinades and sauces** include garlic and herb, chilli, and curry sauce, and Thai style is especially delicious. Another easy win is mustard sauce, easily made by mixing a good helping of mild mustard with some soured cream or crème fraiche to smother over your fish.
- **Fish pie and fishcakes** are winners for those who hate filleting and boning. Just bake a decent-sized fish, allow to cool and then flake off chunks of meat by hand to add to your pie or fishcake mix.

CHAPTER FIVE

FISHING & CULTURE

'Calling fishing a hobby is like calling brain surgery a job.'

PAUL SCHULLERY

'Fishing is not an escape from life, but often a deeper immersion into it.'

HARRY MIDDLETON

'Fishermen are born honest, but they get over it.'

ED ZERN

'Fishing is complete and utter madness.'

SPIKE MILLIGAN

Few other pastimes stir such obsession as angling. Whether it is the vast array of skills and techniques, the vivid characters it attracts, or just the endless mystery of water, our sport is rich. Besides great anglers, mighty fish spawn their very own legends, and angling has an incredible treasury of books, tales and folklore. You only have to spend some time in the company of any seasoned angler to hear a story or three, and while you might fully expect a degree of exaggeration, some of the most remarkable accounts of all time are perfectly true.

What we cannot hope to capture in these pages is the full richness of global angling culture. Everywhere you travel in the world, fishing is the same and yet uniquely different. From the basic premise of hook and line, anglers have tinkered and refined to create an infinite variety of methods. Whether it's dry fly fishing for trout or trolling for saltwater giants, certain techniques attain cult status.

Perhaps it's not so surprising, therefore, that angling is considered an art as much as a hobby, or that Izaak Walton described it as 'the contemplative man's recreation' and something that 'can never be fully learned'. Our final section is therefore a celebration of broader fishing culture, from incredible methods and catches, to classic books, myths and echoes in the very language we speak. Sadly, we couldn't hope to cram in every incredible story or notable angler, but we'll take a whistle stop tour of highlights from around the globe.

FOLKLORE

THE SALMON OF KNOWLEDGE

Many generations have marvelled at the salmon's uncanny powers of navigation, which were once attributed to a mystical inner wisdom. Irish legend tells of the 'Salmon of Knowledge', a fish that gained all the world's learning by eating hazelnuts that dropped from a magic tree.

The poet Finegas spent seven years fishing for the salmon, and when he finally caught it, he asked his servant, Fionn, to cook it. However, while checking to see if supper was ready, Fionn accidentally burned his thumb. As soon as he sucked it, he started to gain the salmon's wisdom. His master then noticed a strange glow in the boy's eyes, and angrily asked if he'd tasted the fish. When he was told of the accident, however, he let the boy eat the whole thing, and for the rest of his life, Fionn could answer any question just by biting his thumb. The young man went on to become leader of the Fianna, a mythical band of Irish heroes.

FINLAND'S EPIC PIKE

With their impressive size and primeval appearance, pike have long inspired monster myths. In Finnish legend, these giant fish are associated with witchcraft and were said to be able to travel to Tuonela, the underworld. In the *Kalevala*, Finland's national epic poem, the hero Ilmarinen is challenged to catch a giant pike without rod or net as a test to win a maiden's hand in marriage. He does so with the help of a giant eagle, but the bird leaves only the head of the beast, much to his frustration.

Later in the saga, three heroes must defeat a pike so immense that it makes their boat run aground. One of the warriors, Väinämöinen, finally slays it and salvages its huge jawbone to create a magic harp. The instrument makes such an enchanting sound, all living things are charmed by it, with even the gods compelled to listen.

FAIRIES AND FURRY TROUT

Japanese myth has it that the world sits on the back of a giant trout. One of the Gods of Fortune, or Ebisu, is sometimes depicted as one of these fish, while legends of the Ainu people of northern Japan and southeastern Russia tell of trout large enough to eat animals and even people.

In Ireland 'The White Trout' is the tale of a fairy spirit in piscatorial form. A callous soldier scoffs at talk of this, and decides to catch and eat it, but when he tosses the fish into a pan and pricks it with a knife, it gives a horrible, human scream. Suddenly, the trout becomes a maiden, bleeding where she was cut. The spirit makes the now terrified soldier renounce his evil ways and release her back into the lake. Here, she regains her freedom, but from that day and forever more, trout will bear a red mark.

Moving north to Iceland, the *Lodsilungur* is said to be a furry trout created by evil spirits to punish the wicked. These tales also have echoes in American folklore about fish that grow a woolly layer to keep them warm in ice-cold waters. Another version of events blames a travelling salesman for spilling hair tonic into the Arkansas River! Various museums and exhibits have displayed bizarre 'furry trout' over the years, but in reality these fish had fungal growths and not magical knitwear.

EXTRAORDINARY EELS

With an even more mysterious life cycle than salmon, and vast migration routes, eels have spawned many myths and superstitions. Aristotle proposed that they didn't reproduce like other fish but slithered from the earth itself, while Māori fables claimed they fell from the sky.

While eels are a delicacy to Europeans, Pacific Islanders see them as sacred creatures, keeping them in spring-fed pools where they become tame and reach huge proportions. According to legend, Maui, a Polynesian figure similar to Hercules, battles a giant eel after finding it in bed with his wife.

In one version of the story, Maui hacks the creature in half. The head then becomes all the freshwater eels in the world, while the tail divides into all the saltwater eels.

LUCKY CARP AND CHINESE DRAGONS

In East Asia, carp have long been seen as a symbol of luck and prosperity, whether you find them basking in temple pools or tattooed to a bicep. In Japanese, *koi,* the word for carp, means romantic love. To the Chinese, the carp represents fortitude and perseverance, in part owing to its connection to the Yellow River, where these fish navigate strong currents and rocky passes. According to legend, when a great fish leapt over the Dragon Gate in the Longmen Mountains, it was transformed into a dragon. (It is a good fit, given the carp's metallic scales and whiskers.)

FEATS OF FORTUNE, CALAMITY & SKILL

A BILLION-TO-ONE HOOK-UP?

The luckiest hook-up in history probably goes to Norway's Kim Vegard Sunde. One day, while trolling for salmon, he connected with a large fish, only to be astonished as it reached the boat. He hadn't hooked it in the mouth at all, but through the split ring of another angler's broken-off lure! If that wasn't crazy enough, it was a virtually identical match in colour and design to the lure he was using.

SCHOOLBOY'S LUCKY PERCH

One of angling's great charms is that fortune can make even a novice into a record breaker. Back in 2002, English schoolboy Dean Rawlings had the shock of a lifetime when fishing a small pond using a bunch of maggots on crude tackle. As he was reeling in, a huge perch flung itself at the bait, and he landed a then British record of 5lb 9oz (2.5kg!)

TWO RECORDS IN A DAY

What are the chances of two records within hours? Indianapolis angler William Garvey was both incredibly lucky and unlucky on a bizarre 1984 trip. Thrilled to catch a record-shattering 5lb 2oz (2.3kg) white bass on Bull Shoals Lake, his piece of history didn't even last the day, as his boat partner William Wilson netted a 5lb 4oz (2.4kg) fish. Unlike Garvey's record of mere hours, Wilson's stood unbroken for over 20 years.

PUT TO THE SWORD!

In 1976 an Australian angler narrowly escaped death after a long battle with a giant swordfish. Just as his huge, black marlin looked beaten, it leapt powerfully up the side of the boat and its bill pierced him clean through, just below the shoulder. Within minutes, he was covered in blood and only avoided death thanks to the captain hastily using an old shirt to bandage him. In spite of a lengthy hospital visit, he was back fishing under a year later. Such incidents are rare but can be fatal: a swordfish killed an Indonesian surfer in 2024.

DEATH BY CATFISH

Should you ever hook a truly gigantic fish, it is vital to have your drag set properly and to keep your line tidy. This lesson was learned too late by a supremely unlucky angler fishing near Vienna in 2000, who hooked a huge catfish only to become entangled in his own line and dragged to his death.

ANGLING WORLD RECORDS

The largest recorded saltwater fish ever caught on rod and line was a great white shark of 3,427lb (1,554kg), landed by legendary Captain Frank Mundus and his mate Donnie Braddick, in 1986. Mundus is said to be the inspiration for Captain Quint in the movie *Jaws*.

The largest-ever officially recorded freshwater fish caught on rod and line was a 661lb (300kg) freshwater stingray, landed in Thailand in 2023. However, in July 2021, a white sturgeon landed from Canada's Frazer River was estimated at over 800lb (363kg). While we'll never know the exact weight, it measured 11ft 6in (3.5m)!

The record for the most fish caught in 24 hours is held by Jeff Kolodzinski of Illinois, who caught 2,469 in a fundraiser for the Fishing For Life charity in 2019.

The longest-ever cast with a rod, line and sinker was 313yd (286.2m), set in 2004 by Belgian surf-casting expert Danny Moeskops.

The longest-ever cast with a fly rod was 78yd (71.3m), set by Steve Rajaff of the USA in 2009.

AMAZING ANGLING CONTESTS WORLDWIDE

While most of us fish for sheer pleasure, anglers have compared catches ever since our distant ancestors first set up a hook and line. Whether it's a big jackpot or just local pride at stake, there is a delicious extra thrill to catching fish in the heat of competition.

The rules of battle vary greatly worldwide. The winner can be decided on total weight or length of fish, by total catch or the best individual specimen. The only certainty is that anywhere you find anglers, you'll find rivalry. However, another given is our sport's great camaraderie, and testing your ability with others is a great way of making new pals besides sharpening skills.

Aside from the usual 'catch what you can in a day' affairs, different angling cultures worldwide have produced some truly unique events. Here are some of the biggest and weirdest.

A COOL ONE MILLION
Drawing crowds of over a million anglers and spectators, South Korea's Hwacheon Ice Trout Festival must be the world's biggest ice-fishing event. Armed with ice drills and blankets besides school-ruler length rods, entrants of all ages target trout, which are stocked in their tens of tons. No need to pack a cooler for your catch!

DRINK LIKE A FISH!
While most angling matches strictly forbid intoxication, Belgium's Booze Trophy positively encourages it. Competitors must drink constantly while trying to fill their nets, risking disqualification if they are too sober. The results are predictably messy, and anyone who can remember much was probably cheating!

BIG BUCKS AND BASS
The world's biggest sport fishing jackpot has to be the USA's Bassmaster Classic. Billed as the 'Superbowl of bass fishing', the top names walk away with over US $1 million (about £745,000) in prize money.

South Korea's Hwacheon Ice Trout Festival

A CROWDED FIELD

As for the most claustrophobic fishing contest, China wins hands down. Events like the China Fishing Club Union Cup host over a thousand anglers, sat just a rod length apart, to catch carp. With top prizes equivalent to several years' salary, competition is fierce.

BETTER NOT LOSE THAT FLY!

If you've ever cursed at getting snagged, spare a thought for competitors at England's The One Fly event. Held annually on the legendary River Test, entrants must choose just a single artificial fly for the day; lose that and it's game over!

CLASSIC BOOKS

The sport of fishing has spawned many, many books. Here are a handful of must-read volumes for your collection.

THE COMPLEAT ANGLER (IZAAK WALTON & CHARLES COTTON, 1653)

A mixture of angling lore, practical advice and verse, this remarkable work is one of the most reprinted books in the English language. It remains a quirky and fascinating glimpse into an earlier age, even if some of the techniques and ideas are amusingly dated.

THE OLD MAN AND THE SEA (ERNEST HEMINGWAY, 1952)

If you described it as the greatest man versus fish tale of all time, few would argue against you. Describing the epic battle between lifelong angler, Santiago, and a giant marlin, this classic of sporting fiction dives into themes of faith, perseverance and the angler's deep connection with the ocean.

TROUT BUM (JOHN GEIRACH, 1986)

A book that didn't just define a sport, but a lifestyle, *Trout Bum* details one man's obsession with fly fishing and love for rivers. Funny, honest and confessional in style, it is among the most relatable angling books ever written, offering a warts-and-all account of why we love to fish.

CASTING AT THE SUN (CHRIS YATES, 1986)

Wise, witty and eccentric, Chris Yates is one of Britain's best-loved angling writers of all time. This work, which many fans rate as their favourite, takes the reader from the magic of childhood fishing to spellbinding encounters at Redmire, a legendary carp lake, and the capture of his inspirational British record fish.

THE LONGEST SILENCE (THOMAS MCGUANE, 1999)

This stirring, beautifully written book evokes one man's lifetime in angling. Besides majestic passages on rivers and fish, it also opens several intriguing cans of worms, tackling subjects such as why we are drawn to different fishing styles, and even the sticky question of why some anglers are less than honest.

TROUT FISHING IN AMERICA (RICHARD BRAUTIGAN, 1961)

A zany, utterly surreal ride, this adventure veers about as far from the beaten trail as fishy literature can get. Swerving between real and imagined places across rural America, it is wonderfully wild and funny. If you've ever pondered how you might dispatch a trout using booze, or whether it's possible to confuse an old lady with a river, this gloriously bonkers book is for you.

MOVIES & TV

Given the huge popularity of fishing, it's surprising so few great movies have been angling themed. Nevertheless, there have been some memorable exceptions to that rule, alongside a handful of cult TV series. Here are some favourites to track down.

A RIVER RUNS THROUGH IT (ROBERT REDFORD, 1992)

A movie so epic, it led to a real-life boom in viewers taking up angling. Based on Norman Maclean's novel, it contrasts the two sons of a fly-fishing minister, and the integral part the sport plays in their lives. Along with stunning Montana scenery, even the casting reeks of authenticity. Lacking water near his home in central LA, it's said Brad Pitt did much of his fly-rod practice on top of a building!

SALMON FISHING IN THE YEMEN (LASSE HALSTROM, 2011)

Following an eccentric sheikh's desire to bring game fishing to his desert homeland, this movie follows a wild plan to achieve the impossible. The real magic is the chemistry between city slicker Harriet (Emily Blunt) and fisheries nerd Dr Alfred Jones (Ewan McGregor), although there are also musings on angling as an act of faith, and even how the perfect cast might save a life.

MENDING THE LINE (JOSHUA CALDWELL, 2022)

Experiencing mental-health difficulties after military service, ex-marine Colter (Sinqua Walls) is prescribed fly fishing as therapy, under hard-bitten mentor Ike Fletcher (Brian Cox). It's not only a great tale of unlikely friendship, but also a movie that might make you look at angling in a whole new light.

FISHING WITH JOHN (JOHN LURIE, 1991)

Featuring a host of famous guests from Dennis Hopper to Tom Waits, this show retains a cult following for its offbeat humour and authenticity, epitomised by the dreamy theme music and wacky locations. Angling tends to make even the most intense people relax, and that is exactly how this series draws out its star guests. You can catch it on YouTube.

A PASSION FOR ANGLING (1993)

The definitive British angling series captures duo Chris Yates and Bob James in their watery element. With some of the most evocative angling footage ever shot thanks to film-maker Hugh Miles, it features beautiful settings, epic fish, eccentric humour and spellbinding narration from Bernard Cribbins. Never bettered.

RIVER MONSTERS (2009–17)

Former science teacher Jeremy Wade is an adventurer whose love of monster fish takes him across the globe to uncover the truth about legendary beasts from arapaima to alligator gar. Where other presenters are full of hype and hyperbole, Wade is wonderfully understated, letting his knowledge and the fish do the talking.

ANGLING LEGENDS

The list of innovative and inspirational people to have changed fishing forever is a long one. Here are just a handful of the true greats worth looking up.

IZAAK WALTON (1593–1683) AND CHARLES COTTON (1630–87)
The two friends who wrote *The Compleat Angler*, fishing's biggest book of all time, are still revered for their impact over 370 years later.

DAME JULIANA BERNERS (1388–1460) could be described as fishing's original influencer, writing the sport's first-ever English language book of significance, *A Treatise of Fishing with an Angle*, circa 1420, and setting down fly patterns and advice that stood for centuries.

Izaak Walton

DICK WALKER (1918–85) A true all-rounder, widely regarded as the 'godfather of modern angling' in Britain and beyond. A record-breaker, author and inventor of flies and tackle, he pioneered a scientific approach and contemporary fishing methods, including specialised fishing for large carp. He inspired countless anglers.

ZANE GREY (1872–1939) Prolific American writer and globetrotter who was instrumental in establishing the sport of big game fishing, smashing several world records in the process.

THADDEUS NORRIS (1811–77) Known as the 'American Izaak Walton' or simply Uncle Thad by countless readers, Norris was the most important fishing writer of his generation. His seminal *American Angler's Book* was also ahead of its time in promoting angling as a healthy, meditative sport, and conservation.

FREDERIC HALFORD (1844–1914) A hugely influential British fly fisher, he refined the technique of upstream dry fly fishing on England's chalk streams, developing a form of angling that retains a cult following to this day.

G.E.M. SKUES (1858–1949) An author and innovator who pioneered using sinking flies, or nymphs, to catch trout. Controversial among the purists of his day, he challenged dogma and elitism in fly fishing and made the sport more accessible.

LEFTY KREH (1925–2018) A lifelong angler, photographer and pioneer of lure fishing and saltwater fly fishing. Among modern angling's first true superstars, he shared his love of the sport through countless articles, while also inventing classic flies such as Lefty's Deceiver.

LEE WULFF (1905–91) Great American fly-fishing author, artist and conservationist. His enlightened attitude to the sport helped establish catch and release angling and efforts to preserve Atlantic Salmon populations.

FRED BULLER (1926–2016) Hugely influential British all-rounder and author, who excelled at every style of fishing from from match to predator angling. He was also an important angling historian.

FISHING FOR WELL-BEING

Anglers have long known that the sport is about so much more than just catching fish. A famous ancient proverb even declares: 'the gods do not deduct from man's allotted span the hours spent fishing'. Perhaps not so far-fetched when you consider growing scientific evidence that angling boosts our physical and mental health – to the extent that some health practitioners in the UK and Europe have started prescribing fishing for its therapeutic value.

- A 2019 study by Anglia Ruskin University showed that anglers had 'significantly lower' levels of anxiety compared to non-anglers, and that for those with severe mental-health challenges, the sport significantly reduced risks of self-harm and suicide.
- The Blue Space therapy enjoyed by anglers has similar benefits to being in the countryside, but with even more advantages, studies show. Increased sunlight and cleaner air tend to be found by water, while the 2013 paper 'Happiness is Greater in Natural Environments' (Mackerron & Mourato), detailed the 'restorative effect' of water, with anglers and other recreational water users achieving 'health by stealth'.
- Charitable groups across the world have used angling as an activity to promote well-being, as it has a positive effect on many people, from those recovering from cancer to PTSD sufferers and the socially isolated.

ANGLING-RELATED WORDS & SAYINGS

To angle for/fish for Refers to the act of subtly trying to get something without asking directly, whether we 'angle' for a pay rise or a compliment.

To be fooled hook, line and sinker Another obviously angling derived phrase, meaning to be totally duped by a trick or con.

To get a rise or bite from The act of deceiving someone or provoking anger, which originates from the angler's craft of trying to get a fish to take a real or artificial bait or fly.

Hooked To be addicted or compelled to keep doing something, whether helpful or harmful.

The one that got away A prospective job, opportunity or love interest that you missed out on.

Plenty more fish in the sea Another way of saying 'there are lots of other chances to get what you want', most often with regard to romance.

To reel someone in To persuade, convince or get somebody to go along with something, whether honest or not.

Trolling The online practice of trying to upset or get a reaction out of others originates from the fishing method of the same name. In less cynical times, trolling simply meant trailing a lure or bait behind a moving boat.

HOW TO WISH ANOTHER ANGLER GOOD LUCK

Tight lines! (US, UK and English-speaking countries) This refers to the fact that keeping a tight line tends to lead to fewer tangles and lost fish.

Sh*tfisk! (Norway) Wishing someone terrible fishing is not unique to Scandinavia, with many cultures believing it bad luck to directly wish someone good luck.

Polamania Kija! (Poland) Another example of reverse logic, this literally means 'break a rod!'.

Petri Heil! (Germany, Austria and Switzerland) This popular saying in German refers to St Peter, the patron saint of fishermen.

USEFUL WEBSITES

UK

anglingtrust.net England's most important fishing organisation. Campaigning for all anglers, it hosts events, fights pollution and other threats, while members also get exclusive tackle and bait discounts.

fallonsangler.net Has a treasury of news, stories and more, including podcasts, book reviews and evocative angling films.

dgfishing.co.uk The author's site has a lively regular blog, fishing videos and more, including books and photography!.

www.anglingtimes.co.uk The online home of Britain's longest-running fishing weekly. Always worth a visit for the latest news, tips and catches.

www.fishingmuseum.org.uk An online collection of fishing history and culture. From the origins of various items of tackle to forgotten anglers who changed the sport forever, it's a fine mixed catch.

USA

asafishing.org The home of the American Sportfishing Association is well worth a visit for US anglers. Working with 800+ organisations, the ASA works hard to protect and promote fishing rights across the country.

flylordsmag.com Champions original storytelling with a host of lively fly-fishing writers. The site contains a ton of great tips, inspiring adventures and evocative photography to fuel your next trip.

www.ginkandgasoline.com Puts the fun into fly fishing in style. Offbeat, original and firmly against stuffiness in angling, it's packed with entertaining and practical content.

www.keepfishwet.org A must-visit site for the conservation-minded angler. Packed with fascinating science studies and practical catch and release tips.

International

igfa.org The home of the International Game Fishing Association. Check out the website for an excellent game fish ID and world records section, besides guidance on what to do should you catch a world-class fish.

USEFUL BOOKS

***Falkus and Buller's Freshwater Fishing* (1975)**
An oldie, but gold for anyone interested in British and European fish and fishing. The level of depth and detail from two legendary anglers is staggering, with a huge amount on history and biology, besides good, solid fishing tips and revealing archive material. Various editions exist, meaning it's always available second hand, and still well worth a read.

***Fishing for Dummies* (Schwipps, Kaminsky, Garnett, 2012)**
Perfect for the novice, this book is an accessible and practical guide to fishing from scratch. Whether the reader wants to try bait or lure angling, on a small stream or out at sea, it unpacks a ton of useful information in user-friendly style. Separate US and UK editions exist, tackling different scenarios and fishing cultures.

***Haynes Fly Fishing Manual* (Bowler, 2016)**
While we could single out many different books on specific types of fly fishing, this is among the most thorough and wide-ranging volumes ever written. Dealing with everything from trout streams to saltwater basics, mayflies to Muddler Minnows, it's extremely practical and clearly illustrated.

***The Pocket Guide to Fishing Knots* (Owen, 1998)**
Given how vital reliable knots are in angling, it's surprising how many of us stick to just two or three old favourites, even where others exist to offer far better strength and presentation. This book, still readily available, covers options for fly, lure and bait fishing alike, including specialist knots for the most demanding scenarios.

***Pocket Guide to Matching the Hatch* (Lapsley and Bennett, 2010)**
Even for experienced fly fishers, bug life can be bewlidering. This great little book is a pocket-sized solution to identifying various caddis, mayflies and other species. Not only does it give lots of practical ID advice, it even gives an 'actual size' key for flies along with advice on artificial copies to use. A real headache solver for anyone with an interest in imitative fly fishing.

***Ultimate Fishing Adventures: 100 Extraordinary Fishing Experiences from Around the World* (Gilbey, 2012)**
Taking in 100 incredible destinations from around the world, this is a book for day dreamers and vacationers with a passion for adventure! While you'd need a big bank balance to cover the whole list, there's lots of scope here for the footloose angler, whether your thing is epic lake trout or spectacular saltwater fishing.

INDEX

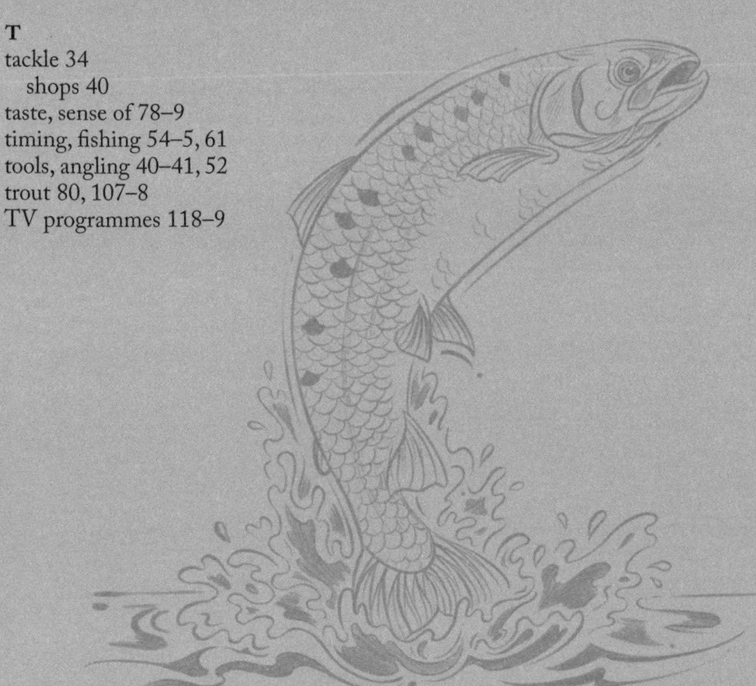

First published 2025 by
Guild of Master Craftsman Publications Ltd,
Castle Place, 166 High Street, Lewes, East Sussex BN7 1XU, UK
www.gmcbooks.com

ISBN 978-1-78494-720-0

The EEA authorised representative is Authorised Rep Compliance Ltd,
Ground Floor, 71 Baggot Street Lower, Dublin, DO2 P593, Ireland
www.arccompliance.com

A catalogue record for this book is available from the British Library.

PUBLISHER Jonathan Bailey
PRODUCTION Jim Bulley
SENIOR PROJECT EDITOR Susie Behar
EDITOR Cath Senker
DESIGN MANAGER Robin Shields
DESIGNER Michael Whitehead
ILLUSTRATOR Alejandra Penaloza

Colour origination by GMC Reprographics
Printed and bound in China